PLANTATION HOUSES
of Curaçao

Jewels of the Past

Photography: Ton Verkuijlen, Brett Russel et al. | *Text:* Jeannette van Ditzhuijzen, Michael A. Newton, François van der Hoeven and Carel de Haseth | A publication of Stichting Curaçao Style in collaboration with Stichting LM Publishers.

GOVERNOR'S PREFACE

Curaçao distinguishes itself from most Caribbean destinations by its rich history and well-preserved cultural heritage. Besides the town of Willemstad, which is registered on the UNESCO World Heritage List, this is nowhere more evident than in the extensive collection of plantation houses that can be found throughout the island. With salient names such as Knip, Pannekoek, Suikertuintje or Santa Barbara, these buildings are of great value to every Curaçaoan.

Because the plantation houses were mostly built on hills, they are easily discernible in the landscape. Due to their often striking colors and distinctive architecture, they are undeniably a significant part of the Curaçao landscape. They are not only sites with a historical meaning, but also places where the past and the present come together. It is a past in which slavery played a prominent role and which is still visible today.

The development of the oil industry at the beginning of the last century and its accompanying industrialization happened at the expense of the work on the plantations and heralded the decline of many plantation houses. In contrast to the past, the present appreciation of the plantation houses has increased considerably. Most of the houses have been beautifully restored, partly as a result of the growing awareness that they are not only beautiful buildings from the past, but that they are also of great economic importance for the present and the future.

Many plantation houses have been repurposed. Some are open to the public as tourist attractions, while others house an art gallery, restaurant or bed and breakfast. A few are privately inhabited. In their various capacities, the plantation houses occupy an important place in Curaçao society and form a significant attraction for tourists visiting the island.

By means of this beautiful collection of photographs you will be taken on a journey through the past and present, while at times being afforded a glimpse of the future of all of the plantation houses in Curaçao. This book is a standard reference work that Curaçao can be proud of. I wish the reader of this book much inspiration and enjoyment.

Lucille George-Wout
Governor of Curaçao

MASHA DANKI

Curaçao has a large number of plantation houses. Their historic architecture is unique due to the use of European, especially Dutch, building styles which were adapted to local tropical construction methods and available building materials.
With the arrival of the oil industry at the start of the last century, the socio-economic structure of Curaçao changed drastically in just a few decades. Of the more than 150 original plantation houses only 78 remain. The rest have disappeared or fallen into ruin. Fortunately, a number of plantation houses have been preserved. Some have become magnificent residences while others have been given new functions, ranging from restaurants, boutique hotels, office spaces, and museums to art galleries. Monumentenzorg Curaçao (the Curaçao Heritage Foundation) was established in 1954. In that year, the Foundation restored the Brievengat plantation house and saved it from demolition. Ten years later, the Ascencion plantation house was also restored. The Foundation's work did not stop there. In recent restorations architects have often made use of contemporary additions. Hopefully, people will understand and appreciate these additions. We no longer live in the nineteenth century and architecture is not a static thing. Our task is, first and foremost, to preserve and safeguard our architectural and cultural heritage for posterity.

In the past sixty years three authoritative texts dedicated to the Curaçao plantation houses have appeared , namely De Monumenten in Woord en Beeld by prof. Dr. M.D. Ozinga (1959), Architektuur en bouwwijze van het Curaçaose landhuis by Michael A. Newton (1986, reissued in 1990), and Landhuizen van Curaçao by Dolf Huijgers (1982). A revised edition of the latter title, written with Lucky Ezechiëls, appeared in 1992. The objective of the Curaçao Style Foundation is to expand our cultural heritage as widely as possible, and so it is considered important that, after almost thirty years, a new book about the plantation houses should appear. With the publication of this book, the Curaçao Style Foundation is celebrating its twentieth anniversary. Thanks to the expertise of its many collaborators, it has become possible to offer a comprehensive overview, in words and in images, of all the plantation houses that have been preserved as jewels from the past. For many it is not entirely clear what exactly constitutes a plantation house. Michael Newton provides clarity on this matter and describes the typical characteristics of these structures. Jeannette van Ditzhuijzen set out in search of historically established facts and anecdotes relating to all 78 still existing plantation houses. The photographers Ton Verkuijlen and Brett Russel treat the reader to an exceptional journey of discovery, visually supplemented at times by others. Carel de Haseth provided vibrant interviews with current and former plantation house residents. Together with Gerda Gehlen and Anita de Moulin, De Haseth reviewed the entire text for historical validity. François van der Hoeven, along with the other members of the Curaçao Archeology Project, managed to locate and record all of the ruins and foundations of lost plantation houses. Some of their experiences have been recorded in this book with the help of photographs taken by Anita de Moulin, Michèle van Veldhoven and Carel de Haseth. We hope to reach as wide an audience as possible with the translation of this book into English by Esty da Costa and into Papiamentu by Lucille Berry-Haseth. Dolf Huijgers, masha danki for your idea and contribution to the Papiamentu edition of this book.

We, board members of the Curaçao Style Foundation, would like to express our gratitude to all of these collaborators and the current owners and residents of the plantation houses. We would also like to thank the many others who generously provided leads, suggestions, and photographs. We would also like to express our gratitude to the sponsors of the first publication of the Curaçao Style Foundation, since, without their support in 1998, it would not have been possible to raise funds for the subsequent publications.

We have all enjoyed working on this publication and hope that future generations will continue to be equally passionate about the preservation of these jewels.

Anko van der Woude   chairman Curaçao Style Foundation
Randolph van Eps   secretary
Johan Schimmel   treasurer
Nicole Henriquez   board member
Lusette Verboom   board member
Ellen Spijkstra   board member, project coordinator

Curaçao, November 2019

TABLE OF CONTENTS

PROCLAMATION.

THE GOVERNOR,

To the affranchised population of Curaçao and dependencies.

In the month October of last year has been proclaimed in your Island the law by which it pleased His Majesty, our most gracious King, to decree that on the 1st of July 1863 slavery should for ever be abolished in Curaçao and its dependant Islands.

That happy day is now there.

From off this moment you are free persons and you enter into society as inhabitants of the colony.

Most heartily do I congratulate you with the blessing bestowed on you by the paternal care of the King; sincerely you may rejoice in the same, but you must also make yourself worthly of this benefit.

In your previous state you have always distinguished yourself by a quiet, orderly behaviour and obedience to your former masters; now as free persons, I am fully confident of it, you will orderly and subordinate to the government perform your duty as inhabitants of the colony, working regularly for fair wages, which you may dispose of at your pleasure, to provide for yourself and your family.

The government will attend to your interest and promote the same as much as possible.

If you require advice address yourself to the District-commissary of your district or to any of the other competent authorities, they shall assist you in every thing which may tend to promote your wellbeing.

Curaçao the 1st of July 1863.

J. D. CROL.

PROKLAMASHON (1 di Yüli 1863-2003)

Proclamation (July 1, 1863-2003)

Pa bondat di Reino
Ami Gran Poderoso
Sin remordimiento
Di kulpabilidat
Den ningun ladronisia
Den negoshi humano,
Sin mi kurason bati
Ta regalá boso awe
Sin kobra un sèn chikí
Pa tur e bondat
Durante dos siglo,
Ku forsa inmediato
Boso LIBERTAT

Kòrda semper si
Ku ta Yu boso tabata
I Yu boso ta keda
Te dia galiña Gueni
Saka djente di koper
Pone webu di oro
Den nèshi kolonial
Di kouchi hulandes

From the goodness of my heart
I, the Powerful One,
Of the righteous Kingdom
Grant you this day,
Without remorse
Without guilt
About any theft
Perpetrated
In the course of human trade,
Without palpitations
Without charging a single cent
Out of the goodness
Shown in the course of two centuries
As of this moment
Your FREEDOM.

Remember always that you were Children
And that Children you will remain
Until the day that Guinea hens
Are born with copper teeth
To lay golden eggs
In the colonial nest
Of their Dutch cage.

Translation:
Esty da Costa, *2019*

Elis Juliana, 2003

HISTORY AND ARCHITECTURE OF THE PLANTATION HOUSE

MICHAEL A. NEWTON

| 9

Landhuis Knip

DEFINITION OF A PLANTATION HOUSE

In Curaçao the Dutch term *landhuis* for plantation house is understood to mean something other than the beautiful country retreats one encounters in the Netherlands and other places. The original *kas di shon* (gentleman's house) or *kas grandi* (the big house), as the plantation house is referred to in Papiamentu, is much more like a feudal farm.

It was already noted by Visman[1] that in the Antilles the Dutch term landhuis as the name for a plantation residence did not appear in either the spoken or written language until the twentieth century. Neither in documents nor in literature from the previous centuries is the designation landhuis found. The only terms used were "dwelling", "plantation house" or simply "the house".

One of the first to use the reference landhuis is Dr. H.P. Muller in his 1905 description of Curaçao[2]. In 1911, J.V.D. Werbata applied the name landhuis on his topographical maps of the island. The detailed Werbata maps are therefore, in principle, a decisive factor whether or not the name landhuis is used.

In historical documents, such as plantation deeds of transfer, the presence of a house was hardly ever mentioned. Even when a detailed inventory was drawn up for the sale, the house itself was barely described so it is not always clear whether the house mentioned in the deed is the same as the current plantation house (landhuis) in question.

In addition to the usually grand former plantation houses in Curaçao such as Savonet, San Juan, Knip, or Brievengat, three other categories of country estates are also designated landhuis. Firstly the houses that were built mainly in the nineteenth century on smaller plots of land then called "gardens" and today often called orchards. Examples include Kas Chikitu and Bloemhof. At the time, these did not qualify as full-fledged plantations. Secondly, there are the mostly late nineteenth-century country residences, such as Cerito or Joonchi, built by wealthy businessmen who lived in town. In terms of function, the latter most closely resemble the Dutch concept of a landhuis.

Finally, there is the category of houses that is not included in this plantation house book. These are the houses built outside the city in the second half of the nineteenth or early twentieth century. They are mistakenly referred to as "plantation houses" (landhuis) when, in fact, they are not indicated as such on Werbata's topographic maps. They are stone residences, often with one or more hipped roofs, built on small plots of land outside the city. They have often been given a name, such as Gosie, Francia, or Sabana Baka. It is partly a question of only a few hectares of land which were allotted by the government after the abolition of slavery in 1863.

These were government grounds parceled out and rented to former slaves with the intention that they could sustain themselves by cultivating the land. Many of these rental grounds happen to still exist, especially at Bándariba. Only since the beginning of the twentieth century has government-owned land been issued on leasehold.

LOCATION

The location of the Curaçao plantation houses varies greatly. Some of them, such as the Zorgvlied and Pos Spaño plantation houses, are situated some eighty meters above sea level, while others, such as Daniel, are located on a vast plain or, as is the case with Zuurzak, in a valley.

In general, however, it can be said that the highest possible elevation on the plantation or garden was sought for the construction site of the plantation house in order to provide the best possible view of the grounds and to take advantage of the refreshing easterly trade winds. As a result, the residence was not always centrally located on the plantation.

Another consideration in the choice of location may have been, especially in the case of plantations far from town, the possibility of visual contact with the surrounding plantation houses. In the event of riots or other dangers, residents could then warn each other with the help of signals such as torches. High in the top façades, according to Visman, would have been hooks designed especially for this purpose, on which people could hang the torch from the upper story window.[3] He presents the valley of Sint Marie (Willibrordus and surroundings) as a prime example of the visual contact between the plantation houses. Here at least ten plantation houses were proximate.

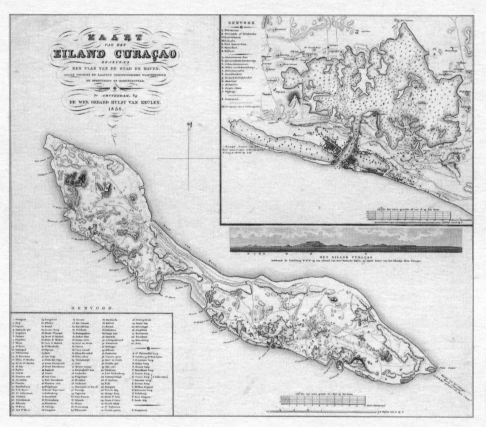

Map issued by the widow of Gerard Hulst van Keulen, 1836

benevens een plan van de stad en haven).[7] This is a detailed map of the island issued in 1836 by the widow Gerard Hulst van Keulen in Amsterdam. On this map, more than a hundred plantation houses are numbered and named in the extensive caption.

At the beginning of the twentieth century the island was not faring well. Due to the prevailing drought the prospects for Curaçao's agriculture were bleak. On the initiative of Governor De Jong van Beek en Donk, who had a strong interest in agriculture, work was started in 1904 on the restoration of the dams that had been seriously neglected following emancipation in 1863. In addition, the construction of a large series of new dams increased the water supply for agriculture. It was decided to have the island measured in order to construct the dams where they would be of greatest use.

The previously drawn maps were not detailed enough to be useful. In addition, the height differences and height drops that were so important for the construction of dams were indicated only by vague hues.

In order to assess the island, the topographer J.V.D. Werbata, who was employed by the Topographic Service of the Dutch East Indies, came to Curaçao in 1906 equipped with a complete set of measuring and drawing instruments.[8] Werbata completed his task in 1909 and returned to the Dutch East Indies after training the Curaçaoan Jonckheer so that the latter could map the other islands. The so-called Werbata maps,

PLANTATION HOUSES AND PLANTATIONS ON OLD MAPS

Besides archival documents and literature, historical maps have provided valuable information about plantations and plantation houses. In the course of the past centuries there have been many maps of the island of Curaçao; these were recently published by Renkema[4]. On the seventeenth and eighteenth century maps, however, the individual plantations, and in particular the plantation houses, hardly appear.

The first map of Curaçao that shows most of the plantations and plantation houses is the "Manuscript map of the island of Curaçao" (*Manuscript-kaart van het eiland Curaçao*)[5]. This map, drawn in 1816 and 1817, was made by Captain in the Engineering Corps H.J. Abbring who was stationed in Curaçao from 1816 to 1825. On this map the many plantation houses are marked with a red dot.

In 1826, using Abbring's map as a starting point, a military topographical map was compiled on the basis of a triangulation plan. On this map the correct shape of the island is shown for the first time and the plantation houses and plantations are indicated[6]. The last relevant nineteenth-century map is the "Map of the Island of Curaçao along with a plan of the city and harbor" (*Kaart van het Eiland Curaçao* consisting of eighteen sheets and using a scale of 1:20,000, appeared in early 1911 at J. Smeulders & Co in The Hague. These beautiful, detailed, colored maps have not been surpassed in terms of accuracy by topographical maps produced subsequently.

THE PLANTATION AS ENTERPRISE

In 1499 the Spanish took possession of Curaçao. At that time the only inhabitants were several small groups of Indians belonging to the Caquetio tribe. The Spaniards never thoroughly colonized the island. Most of the Indians were brought to Hispaniola as slaves. The island was, however, used as a trading station for the mainland.

Initially a trading company, the Dutch West India Company (WIC) also attempted to develop the island agriculturally after it took occupation in 1634. At the beginning, agriculture was mainly focused on the export of products such as tobacco, sugar cane, cotton, and indigo.

Shortly after 1634, the WIC began independently cultivating a strip of land around the Schottegat (Rooi Canarie), the valley of Sint Marie and terrain near the Sint Michielsbaai, but from the start of colonization the WIC Lords Governors in the motherland also tried to attract free planters. Anyone who settled on the island in the decades after the capture of Curaçao could be consigned land if they so wished. The concessionaire was thereby obliged to cultivate the soil.

In no time, though, all agricultural production was needed for the island's

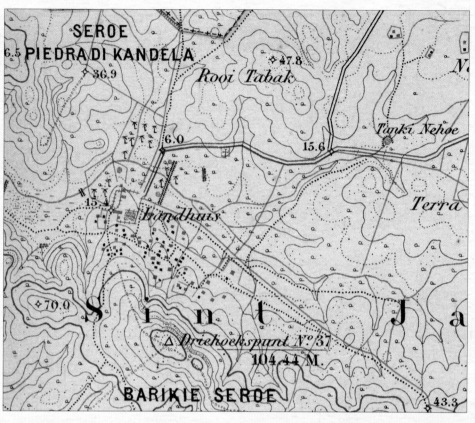

Section of a map by J.V.D. Werbata, 1911

residents and for the enslaved who were brought to Curaçao that had become a slave depot during the second half of the seventeenth century. The cultivation of food crops, mainly corn or sorghum, was important. Trade products for export were therefore always of secondary importance.

Cattle breeding was, however, of great significance for the planters. According to a statement made by the WIC director in 1740, the owners of plantations were totally dependent on the income from livestock farming.

The actual plantation history of Curaçao begins around 1660. From this

period onward, there are two parallel developments: a robust expansion of Company plantations and the emergence of many private plantations. The process of plantation development proceeded at a rapid pace in the late seventeenth and early eighteenth centuries. In 1696 there were already 111 plantations and gardens. Important plantations such as Savonet, Knip, Ascencion, Santa Cruz, San Juan, San Nicolas, Groot and Klein Santa Martha, Spaanse Put, Wacao, Engelenberg (Cas Abou), Siberie, Groot and Klein Sint Joris, and Santa Barbara already existed.[9]

In the early eighteenth century, the management of the Company plantations, such as Oostpunt/Duivelsklip, Koraal

Savonet plantation, 1921

Bell post at Zorgvlied

Tabak, Noordkant, Rooi Canarie, Piscadera, Malpais, Sint Marie, and Hato left much to be desired, and consequently the plantations became neglected. With the exception of Hato, the WIC decided to dispose of its plantations by selling or renting them.

The number of plantations and gardens increased throughout the eighteenth century. In 1817 there were 134 plantations and 131 gardens. However, these numbers began declining, and by 1842 there were only 96 plantations and 39 gardens.[10]

According to Renkema, there are two possible causes for the differences in these figures. In the first place, the district masters had different interpretations of the terms "plantation" and "garden", resulting in inaccurate figures which are difficult to compare. In the second place, several plantations were merged. A merger of two plantations resulted in the redundancy of one of the two plantation houses.

Some of these were therefore either torn down or so neglected that they fell to ruin.

This process continued on a smaller scale throughout the nineteenth century. The number of independently managed plantations therefore declined from 99 (around 1820) to 94 (in 1857) and finally to around 89 (in 1888). With the exception of Choloma and Rio Magdalena, new plantations were not added in the nineteenth century.

The abolition of slavery in 1863 brought about some change in the system of land ownership. Many former slaves continued to live on the plantation and became paid farm workers. For the use of a small parcel of plantation land - where they lived, grew their own food and were able to keep small livestock - they were forced to work for free for a few days a year on the plantation owner's land. This was the so-called *paga-tera* system[11]. In addition, various government lands were parceled out and leased in small plots.

Since the mid-nineteenth century, agriculture has declined in prestige and economic significance. The lowest point was reached at the beginning of the twentieth century. With the arrival of the oil refinery in 1915, many workers moved from the countryside to the refinery, and the plantations diminished in importance. Only a few plantations, such as Savonet, continued to produce until the mid-twentieth century.

THE PLANTATION HOUSE

No buildings have been preserved from the pre-Columbian (Indian) or Spanish periods in Curaçao. All the buildings, including the plantation houses as we know them today, date from the Dutch period.

The plantation house was the plantation's main residence. Usually the owners did not live permanently on the plantation because they often owned businesses in town where they had other homes. In such cases, the plantation was run by a

Savonet plantation complex

manager called the *vitó*. He had his own home near the plantation house.
In those days the grounds around the house were always kept clear of low vegetation such as weeds, cacti and undergrowth. This was done to combat insects. With a dense vegetation the *lembelembe's* (*Drosophila*), a kind of banana fly, could be a real scourge in the early morning and dusk. Near the house was also the *playa*, a piece of land covered by a layer of white coral stones brought in from the coast. The laundry was placed there to dry in the sun. Because the bright sun bleached the wash, so to speak, such a playa was also called a *bliki*.[12] On the plantations where there was actually some form of animal husbandry, agriculture and/or horticulture, there were various other structures in the vicinity of the country house.

ANNEXES

At some plantation houses, separate stables were built for the horses nearby. The remaining cattle, especially goats, roamed free during the day and in the evening were herded into the cattle corrals, walled plots of land some tens of square meters in size.

The products grown on the plantation were stored in storage sheds, unless they were immediately sold in town. These *mangasina's* might be located either in the vicinity of the plantation house or near the area of the plantation where the crop was grown. The maize (sorghum) mangasinas were significant stone structures with a pitched or hipped tiled roof. They can still be seen in many locations although these days the roofs have often collapsed, or the buildings have been given a different function. The threshing floor was near the mangasina. The few plantations that also cultivated or manufactured other products had several storage sheds. The best example of this is Savonet where in the vicinity of the house, apart from the large sorghum shed, there stood smaller mangasinas for products such as divi divi pods, cotton seed, hay, charcoal, lime, milk, and cheese.

Savonet even had a separate workshop for the blacksmith, the forge.

In some cases, the entire plantation was walled in to keep out unwanted guests. An example of this is Fuik where, in the eighteenth century, a wall was built around the spacious 120 x 150 meter complex, within which there were a country house, annexes and mangasinas. The site was accessible via two monumental gates.

In the vicinity of the plantation house there was also the bell which was used to send signals to the slaves and later to the workers. The bell was hung between two hefty columns a few meters high, or suspended from a steel or wooden framework. In the latter case, the framework was often mounted on top of a large stone column that was two to three meters tall and with a diameter of sometimes one meter. Nowadays, the bell frame has usually disappeared and only the column remains standing. In the twentieth century this gave rise to the myth that these were slave poles, such as the one at Zorgvlied, to which the slaves were tied before being punished.

SLAVE VILLAGES

The slaves on the plantations built their own shelters, originally based on African models. Rectangular slave or (later) workers' shelters were built in clusters. These clusters could eventually form a whole village, especially on the vast plantations with many slaves. What is striking is that the houses were often randomly built in relationship to one another. In contrast to the town and its

| 15

Slave village near Siberie

Slave village near Savonet

surroundings where the slave houses were generally made of stone, the dwellings on the plantations were mostly made of small tree trunks, branches and loam, covered by an obliquely rising protective layer of coral or crushed stone that was plastered against the outer walls: these shelters are called *kas di kunuku* or *kas di pal'i maishi*. Stone slave houses are rarely found on the plantation. As far as we know, in the mid-nineteenth century stone slave houses were built only at the Savonet plantation by the plantation owner: a unique slave village of eighteen stone dwellings, laid out in three rows of six houses. After the slaves' emancipation in 1863, many former slaves continued to work and live on the plantation. Many left the plantations only after industrialization. The ones that stayed behind continued to live in the kas di kunuku well into the twentieth century.

WELLS, DAMS, AND ORCHARDS

The plantation houses and some annexes were usually equipped with reservoirs

to which the rainwater for domestic use was channeled and stored via a system of aquaducts. These reservoirs were insufficient for the plantation's pursuits of growing crops and maintaining livestock. Wells were therefore dug for the purpose of obtaining groundwater. The wells which varied in diameter were dug by hand and excavated through the usually hard subsoil. The top of the well was fortified with a round masonry stone edge approximately one meter high. The water was drawn with buckets. Another type of well is the *pos di pia*. This is a partly inclined well, with or without steps, so both people and cattle can walk down to the surface of the water at the bottom.

The water yield of the wells depended on the level of the groundwater. To maintain a certain level, dams were built between water flows or *rooien* in the landscape. When it rained, the water collected on the upstream side of the dam, so that the water could sink into the ground and not flow directly out to sea. These dams were mostly earthen embankments,

but there were also brickwork dams, or combinations of both. There is a particularly large brickwork dam near Pos Monton on the Savonet plantation in the Christoffel Park. It is a dam of approximately three meters high that has five large buttresses.

In the twentieth century most of the dams had disappeared or were poorly maintained, leading to a drop in the groundwater level on these former plantations. In the lower sections of the plantations, especially where the groundwater was high, trees were planted to create orchards: mostly fruit trees but also some shade trees to create a cool environment. Due to the lack of maintenance, most of the orchards on the island have disappeared. The remaining orchards tend to be in poor shape.

WATER AND SALT PLANTATIONS

Spread across the island were plantations with naturally high groundwater levels making water collection easier. The water

16

Salt extraction at San Nicolas

Indigo containers

from these so-called water plantations was transported to town in barrels on donkeys and sold there. During particularly arid periods, when there was hardly any water in the reservoirs, the water from the water plantations was a necessity even though the groundwater was brackish compared to the water from the reservoirs.

Salt pans were installed in the Spanish period. Although salt extraction was also performed in the seventeenth and eighteenth centuries, larger scale harvesting didn't take place until salt plantations were created in the nineteenth century[13] and salt pans were made in the many inland bays on the south coast of the island. Low walls separated the shallow parts of the bays into a series of plots. These salt pans measured approximately 45 by 30 meters, with a maximum depth of 90 cm. At the beginning of the dry period, salt seawater was siphoned into the pans through openings in the walls. The supply ducts were then closed and the sun evaporated

the water. The salt that was thus deposited on the bottom was chopped up, collected, and stored for export. These days the former salt pans in the inner bays can be identified by the walls of the plots that are still partially present.

INDIGO CONTAINERS

In addition to livestock farming and the cultivation of agricultural products for the local market, the WIC also attempted to develop commercial crops such as the indigo plant. From the last quarter of the seventeenth century to the first part of the eighteenth century the island exported the raw blue material for textile dye.

The indigo culture was quite extensive at the time. Indigo was planted on several plantations, and indigo containers, called *bak'i blous*, were built. Although they haven't been used in over three hundred years, there are still remnants of indigo containers on the island. Even more of them are being discovered in remote areas

of former plantations. They are one of the few visible witnesses to the production of crops from the distant past.

The indigo production system consists of three masonry containers made of coral or quarry stone which are gradually arranged one on top of the other. The interiors of these bins, as was often also the case with cisterns, were lined with bricks and subsequently coated with a waterproof layer of plaster. At some locations there are two sets of bins alongside each other.

The branches of the indigo plant were tied together in bunches and compressed under heavy pieces of wood. The "soaking tub" was the upper large water-filled container where all of this indigo fermented for about eighteen hours. Next, the now blue water was spilled over to a lower, second container called the "whipping tub". By stirring and beating the mass with wooden spatulas, the indigo sank to the bottom in little balls. In order to derive as much dye as possible from the blue water, this process was

San Juan plantation house

repeated in an even lower third tank, the "sinking tub". Finally, the blue sediment was scooped out of the trays and dried.

Because substantial amounts of water were required, the bins were situated near wells or other water sources[14]. Due to the considerable stench that was caused by the process, the bins were also usually located on remote parts of the plantation.

ARCHITECTURE

Over the course of the centuries the architectural style of the buildings in historic Willemstad and the houses on the plantations show many similarities. This is especially the case in the architectural façades. The layout of the buildings in town and on the plantations, however, differs considerably. That is understandable because smaller town spaces necessitated more compact buildings whereas there was more open space on the plantations for larger structures.

FLOOR PLANS

The floor plan of the Curaçao plantation house was partly determined by two climatic factors: wind direction and sun. In general the houses have a rectangular floor plan positioned as favorably as possible toward the prevalent easterly winds. The air flow and thereby the pleasantly cooling effect was optimized. In addition to the principal shape of the house, the prevailing wind direction also determined the location of various rooms. Bedrooms, for example, were located as much as possible on the eastern side of the house in order to take advantage of

The attic of Savonet plantation house

the breeze. This was in contrast to the kitchen which was always situated on the western side of the house, away from the wind, so that smoke and cooking odors would be released directly outside without spreading throughout the house. The kitchen could also be situated to the west as a separate building unattached to the house, such as the one at Klein Santa Martha.

Except for isolated cases, the construction period of a Curaçao plantation house is difficult to determine on the basis of the floor plan. Most floor plans recur in the seventeenth, eighteenth, and nineteenth centuries.

To shield the core of the house from the sun, galleries were placed on two or more sides of the building. About seventy percent of the Curaçao country houses have a gallery in one form or another. The galleries are situated either at the front and rear of the main part of the house, on three sides, or completely around the core. Almost half of the plantation houses

have only a front and back gallery. The majority of these plantation houses have an attic above the core of the house. In these cases, the front and rear gallery are usually formed by extending the roof of the core at the front and rear, such as the ones at Savonet, Habaai or Brievengat. In the nineteenth century in particular, as the attic floor gradually disappears, galleries are also formed by separate saddle or shield roofs on the front and rear. This is the case with Klein Piscadera and Papaya respectively.

Approximately seventeen percent of the plantation houses have a core completely surrounded by a gallery, as at Ascencion, Knip, San Juan or Van Engelen. Next, a third of the plantation houses have a floor plan that appears only sporadically, such as Groot Santa Martha's U-shaped floor plan; or a floor plan that even occurs just once, as at Bloemhof; or a floor plan that has become "unclear" due to renovations,which made the original layout no longer recognizable. The core of the plantation house is usually divided

Klein Santa Martha plantation house - Neo-Curaçao Dutch style

Groot Santa Martha plantation house- Curaçao Dutch style

into two or three rooms. The largest room was furnished as a salon or *sala*. The remaining rooms of the core, as well as the separated galleries, had multiple functions. They served as bedrooms or dining rooms, as offices, kitchens or storage areas. The attic was often used only for sleeping or as a storage space. In some plantation houses one can still find the wooden or steel hooks on which hammocks hung. These hooks were fixed in the ceilings or the roof beams, crosswise in the corners of the room.

FAÇADE ARCHITECTURE

In the vast majority of cases, the top façade of the plantation house is the most characteristic feature of the building. As opposed to the floor plan, it is generally possible to determine the period of the house's construction based on the façade shape and the façade details. The shapes that were fashionable at the time of construction are usually also found in the shapes of the dormer windows.

Even if no top façade was used, such as with a hipped roof, the dormer windows can often provide an indication of the construction period of the house. Initially the architectural style of the motherland was copied in the Dutch colonies. This was also the case in Curaçao where, at the start of the Dutch presence, the construction methods and decorative elements from the mother country were still fairly faithfully adopted. Beginning in the eighteenth century in particular, European contours and decorative elements are interpreted and further developed in their own, Curaçaoan way. The availability of building materials and the skills of local craftsmen undoubtedly played a determining role in this development.

ROOF SHAPES

From the seventeenth century onward plantation houses display both saddle and hipped roofs above their core. A saddle roof is enclosed between two top

façades, such as at the Savonet, Ascencion or Habaai plantation houses. A hipped roof has a roof surface on all four sides, such as at the San Juan or Van Engelen plantation houses. Adjacent to the roofs above the cores there are lean-to roofs above the galleries. Because the attic above the core of the house was often also used, these roofs were steep. For optimum ventilation, dormer windows were placed across from each other. The steep hipped roofs, especially those dating from the eighteenth century, were usually also equipped with dormer windows on the ends. In the second half of the nineteenth century, with the advent of neoclassicism, the core and the galleries are often individually fitted with a hipped roof. The spans grow smaller and the roofs become less steep. The useful attics disappear.

BUILDING STYLES

From the seventeenth to the nineteenth centuries, four major building styles

Savonet plantation house - Curaçao baroque

can be distinguished. Determining the start or ending of a style is impossible. In general there are overlaps spanning many decades. Some twenty years ago, in order to distinguish the various architectural styles from the seventeenth to the nineteenth centuries in Curaçao, a number of architectural and art historians on the island gave them the following names.

THE CURAÇAO DUTCH STYLE

The Curaçao Dutch style was popular from the beginning of the Dutch presence in the seventeenth century to the first half of the eighteenth century. This style can be recognized by a simple top façade that is capped by a small triangle (fronton) with a horizontally positioned rectangle below. This rooftop with a classical profile is the only characteristic feature of this style since the rest of the façade is very simple. The style can most clearly be traced back to the Netherlands, where this type of roof, originally stemming

from the Italian Renaissance, was used as early as the sixteenth century. This roof style with a classic profile can be found at the plantation houses of Ascencion and Groot Santa Martha.

CURAÇAO BAROQUE

The entire eighteenth century produced exceptional examples of this architecture. Different types of façades were created, but they all had one feature in common: the curved façade lines in numerous variations which has come to be characterized as Curaçao baroque.

The most famous example of this is the so-called in- and outward swirling façade. In addition, the arched arcade - a row of arches on columns - frequently appears in galleries. In top façades, the curved lines are usually only applied at the core of the building. These are often the most beautiful forms, such as those at the Savonet, Malpais, Habaai, and Zeelandia plantation houses. There are

also plantation houses, however, where the curved lines run the entire width of the façade, such as at Brievengat.

NEO-CURAÇAO DUTCH STYLE

Architecture was much simpler in the first half of the nineteenth century. The façade lines are simple, sloping straight lines (spout façades). The top of the spout façade is seen as a simple derivative of the seventeenth-century Curaçao Dutch style and has therefore been given the name Neo-Curaçao Dutch style.

A ventilation opening for the attic was often provided at the top, sometimes with a decorative shape such as a star around it. These façades are to be found at the Klein Santa Martha and Knip plantation houses.

NEOCLASSICISM

Neoclassicism in Curaçao was strongly influenced by both Europe and the United

Cerito plantation house- neoclassicism

States. Neoclassicism, popular in the second half of the nineteenth century, first came to be used in town between 1850 and 1860, when several large buildings were erected in this new style. It was only later used in the construction of plantation houses and country homes, such as the Ronde Klip and Cerito plantation houses.

Typical of neoclassicism is the symmetry of the façade and the use of cornices. The broad pediment (the triangular surface) on the front of the façade on large columns is also characteristic.

HISTORICAL BUILDING MATERIALS

The building materials that both the Indian and Spanish residents used for their homes were loam and wood. As far as we know, the only stone structure that the Spaniards built was probably a church in the vicinity of Santa Barbara[15]. An important archival document providing insight into the previously used building materials is an overview of both local and imported materials available on the island in the early nineteenth century. This overview, "Explanatory memorandum relating to Building Materials" (*Memorie betrekkelijk de Bouwmaterialen*)[16], was drawn up in 1825 by the first captain-engineer-adjutant Biben during the preparations for the construction of the new fortifications, the Waterfort and the Riffort.

CERAMIC BUILDING MATERIALS: BRICKS AND ROOF TILES

Brick was used from the beginning of the Dutch presence in Curaçao. Usually both the bricks and the roof tiles were transported as ballast on the sailing ships from the motherland. They were not, however, shipped in sufficient quantities, so from the start both imported and local building materials were used side by side. Although there was an irregular and insufficient supply for the construction of all of the brick structures, millions of stones were shipped. Buildings that are made entirely of brick can still be found in the oldest part of Willemstad. Brick, however, was used mainly for the detailing of arches, moldings, gutter edges, dormer windows or the masonry of loopholes which could hardly be executed in the natural stone found locally. Brick was also sometimes used for floors, such as those at the Knip plantation house.

Comparative cost price calculations made by the military engineer Biben show that brick was not only more scarce but also much more expensive than coral or quarry stone. The construction of a brick wall was about six times more expensive than the same construction using quarry stone.

Until the end of the eighteenth century, the brick supplied was, as far as is known, mostly the yellow "ijssel" brick, a light, fairly small-sized brick that was (and is) manufactured in the Gouda area on the Dutch IJssel river. Due to its light weight, the brick was easy to transport. The brick

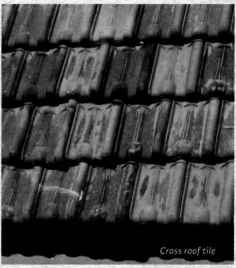

Brick pediment frame

Old Dutch roof tiles

Cross roof tile

was somewhat larger than the current ijssel brick of 16 x 8 x 4 or 5.5 cm. At the end of the nineteenth century the yellow brick was largely displaced by the larger red brick[17]. According to Hartog, bricks were no longer loaded as ballast after the mid-nineteenth century.[18]

Roof tiles were among the building materials imported from the motherland during one of the first supply trips in 1635. The Old-Dutch tiles, originating from the tile factories along the Rhine and the IJssel, came in various designs and colors. Most were red but there were also glazed (dark blue-black) and braised (dull blue-gray) tiles.

Particularly in the nineteenth century other types of tiles were also supplied. Of these, the cross tile (*kruispan*) is the best known and most frequently used on the island because it created a tighter closure than the Old-Dutch tile. Originally this tile was called the Boulet tile or French tile. It was invented in the mid-nineteenth century by Boulet & Cie in Paris and is known in the Netherlands as a cross tile because the tiles were placed in a staggered formation. In 1885 they were advertised for sale in Curaçao as "French tiles, Boulet style".[19] Unique are the zigzag-shaped tiles from Bridgewater that were introduced by the Englishman John Godden around 1880. He ordered these for his phosphate extraction plants at Newport (now the Mining Company) and the manganese mine at Newtown (near Jeremi).

In the nineteenth and twentieth centuries an attempt was made to manufacture roof tiles, including concrete tiles, locally. These have, however, never been produced in large quantities.

CORAL AND QUARRY STONE

Initially, due to a lack of building materials imported from the motherland, the Dutch West India Company was forced to use locally available materials. At first coral was used to replace brick. Soon quarry stone was added.

The designations coral and quarry stone are often used interchangeably, even though there is a marked difference between them. In the past, coral lay strewn along the coast in considerable quantities and was there for the taking. In fact, it is coral debris; remains of dead and broken coral reefs.

Along the coast, including at the Rif in Otrobanda, this coral rubble can still be found. The coral used as a building material comes in many shapes and sizes. Due to the polishing effect of the surf and curves inherent to coral, coral can easily be distinguished from the much rougher and angular quarry stone. In addition, coral is harder than quarry stone. Quarry stone was extracted by carving out or blowing up limestone formations with the help of explosives. This limestone originated in the early Tertiary and Quaternary era (the youngest geological

Zigzag-shaped roof tile

The finishing of the underside of a roof tile with lime

period) when limestone hills and limestone terraces were formed along large parts of the south and north coast, respectively, due to coral being deposited on the older volcanic part of Curaçao.

The use of one or the other type of stone was dependent on the location of the future structure. Coral, which was initially there for the taking, was easier to obtain than quarry stone that had to be mined. However, the transportation costs of large amounts of stone were high. The closer the house was to the sea, the more coral was used. Thus, many houses on Pietermaai and along Penstraat have been built from coral. The buildings located more inland, such as plantation houses, were mainly made of quarry stone.

The coral and quarry stone used was often very irregular in shape. As a result, walls constructed with these types of stone are generally much thicker than walls erected with regularly shaped bricks. Thick walls are much more the result of the shape of the stone than the often heard argument that thick walls were built to keep out the heat.

The thickness of the walls built with coral and quarry stone varies considerably. For homes, thus also for plantation houses, the dimensions vary from approximately 30 cm for non-load-bearing interior walls to 40 to 50 cm for load-bearing (outside) walls. Cisterns often had even thicker walls. In the beginning, the coral was bricked with clay as a mortar. Soon, however, this clay was mixed with lime and possibly sand or completely replaced by lime and sand mortar, which was sometimes supplemented with trass. Due to the irregular shapes of the coral and rubble stone, the walls erected with these types of stone were completely plastered over with lime.

CONCRETE

At the beginning of the twentieth century, the use of coral and quarry stone for construction was slowly being abandoned for concrete blocks and concrete. For the first concrete, which appeared in the 1920s and onward, finger coral was used as aggregate and cement. The concrete was poured in stages by gradually filling timber forms of 20 to 30 cm with this finger coral concrete. When the poured strip hardened, the formwork was raised again and the next layer was poured. This *beton bashá* can sometimes still be recognized by the deposit seams that remained visible even after the wall had been plastered.

LIME AND BURNING LIME

From the start of the Dutch presence, lime, mixed with clay and/or sand, was used as mortar. Lime was mainly used for plastering walls. The undersides of roof tiles were also lubricated with lime to achieve better waterproofing.

The lime was produced in two ways. The oldest and most common method was

containers   Quarry stone   Finger coral with cement

burning lime in a field oven. Much later, at the end of the nineteenth century, in addition to the field oven, the brick-built limekiln came into use. The coral of the coastal reefs and the quarry stone of the low terraces served as raw material; both are a kind of limestone.

The ovens were fired with all kinds of wood, but charcoal and coal were also used as fuel. The latter was used only in the brick oven.

The manchineel tree as well as wreckage from stranded or wrecked ships was widely used as firewood. The number of the island's trees decreased greatly from burning lime. To prevent uncontrolled logging of trees for the limekilns, a regulation was issued in 1826 prohibiting anyone from burning lime without the government's permission. For the plantation owner, however, the burning of lime, especially during the dry periods when he had little work for his slaves, was a welcome addition to his income.

THE FIELD OVEN

The field oven is a fairly primitive limekiln and is designed to be used only once. The dimensions of such a kiln could vary considerably; the size was primarily dependent on the quantity of firewood available.

In 1829, the Reverend Bosch gave, in addition to an extensive explanation of the folklore that accompanied the burning, a precise description of the building of a field oven[20]. The base of the supposedly small limekiln that he had installed on his Zeelandia plantation had a diameter of 24 feet (7.3 m). As horizontally as possible, layer after layer of wood alternating with stone, a sloping, almost five meter (!) high oven was stacked. The bottom layer was always wood; in this case it was five feet (1.5 m) high. A layer of stones, a layer of wood and a final layer of stones were stacked on top of this; respectively they measured a height of 4, 4 and 3.5 feet (1.2, 1.2 and

1 meter). According to the calculations, this limekiln would yield 1,500 bushels (= 43 m³) of slaked lime. In the center of the meters-high pile, there was an opening with a diameter of a few decimeters from top to bottom. Stuffed with strips of firewood, the oven was lit in the middle. The fire was drawn down through the cylindrical opening, so that the kiln started burning from the inside. Only after many hours did it burn fully and the entire structure would become one glowing mass. In places where the oven started to burn too quickly the sides were sprinkled with water. It took several days before the oven burned out completely. The resulting lime deposits were then extinguished, and only the fairly pure "fatty" lime remained.

THE BRICK LIMEKILN

In the early decades of the nineteenth century, some permanent limekilns were also built in Curaçao, Aruba and Bonaire. The larger ovens in Curaçao and Aruba

Limekiln

measured six to eight meters high and were conically shaped hollow structures with a chimney at the top. Both at the bottom and at about two thirds up the side were openings through which one could enter the oven to fill and empty it. There was another hole next to the bottom opening through which the oven was heated and that also served to supply air. An advantage of this type of oven was that it required much less fuel than the field oven did. Both in Curaçao and in Aruba there are (remnants of) brickwork ovens. In Curaçao these remnants are located near the Kima Kalki Marina at Spaanse Water and at the mouths of both the Saliña of Jan Thiel and the Saliña of Rif Sint Marie. The one in Aruba, built in 1892 on the Ranchostraat in Oranjestad, has been reasonably well preserved. In the course of the twentieth century, the locally burnt lime was replaced by the cheaper imported lime and the increasingly popular and also mainly imported cement that was easier to process.

LIME AND PAINT

Because until the beginning of the twentieth century lime has always been used as plaster, originally walls were generally white, and color was used only sporadically. Frames, shutters, windows and doors were often dark green in color.

In 1817, Governor A. Kikkert, at the suggestion of Dr. Benjamin de Sola, determined that the houses in the city district should be given a color to protect the eyes. In the opinion of De Sola, the reflection of the bright sunlight on the white walls caused eye inflammations that could even lead to blindness.[21] Although the above provision only applied to Willemstad and its suburbs, in the subsequent decades various plantation houses also took on a color. This was achieved by adding a colorant to the lime water.

In the publicized regulation, the above was worded as follows: "Since it has been indicated to us by an expert that the white walls of the houses are very detrimental to the sight, owing to the reflection of the sun's rays on the eyes, and thereby causing irreversible weakening of same, it is so that based on the recommendations made to us, we have found it to be for the common good and have judged advisable to command this: that the walls of the houses and other buildings in Willemstad, on the other side of the harbor, on Pietermaay or outside the stone city walls and on Scharlo shall no longer be plastered or washed white; being free to anyone to use such other colors as he or she will choose: anyone that plasters or washes white their houses or buildings after this proclamation will be fined the amount of twenty-five pezos van Agten[22]".

WOOD

Deforestation occurred in Curaçao during both the Spanish and Dutch eras. Many trees were felled for the construction of plantations and for the procurement of firewood to burn charcoal and lime. In addition, until about the end of the nineteenth century, the number of trees diminished greatly due to the felling of commercial types of wood such as Lignum vitae (*wayaká*), mahogany and dyewood (*brasil*). This last type of wood was already an export item under the Spanish occupation and was subsequently sent to the Netherlands by the shiploads, particularly in the seventeenth century where it was used for the preparation of red paint.

As with so many building materials, wood was imported from the motherland in the early days of the Dutch occupation. Soon, however, locally harvested wood was also used. Cactus trees of adequate dimension, for example, could be cut into planks for construction or sawed into wood for window frames.[23]

Wood from the manchineel and mahogany trees was used in construction as well as by the cabinet makers, who were particularly renowned in the nineteenth century, although they increasingly began to import their (mahogany) wood. The vast majority of building and construction timber, however, was supplied from North America as early as the eighteenth century. This was a cheaper and often better quality of wood than that from the Netherlands which was obtaining wood from the Baltic Sea countries at that time. The North American types of wood were mainly yellow pine, similar to pine, and pitch pine. The latter, American pine, was the strongest coniferous wood and was used extensively in construction.

By the beginning of the nineteenth century one just had to specify the kind and size needed, and then the wood was sent ready-made from America. One could even (at that time) order fully prefabricated wooden houses.

Hardwood like mahogany was occasionally imported from areas in the region such as Santo Domingo, Jamaica and Colombia. Due to the limited possibilities for local exploitation, the shoddy transport and the irregular supply, this type of wood was relatively more expensive than the North American kind.

Lime plaster on wood

In addition to the roof tiles already described, wooden shingles must have also been used as roofing material in Curaçao during the seventeenth and eighteenth centuries. They are mentioned in old documents and descriptions. Around the mid-nineteenth century these wooden shingles, however, were no longer in use.

KAS DI KUNUKU

As described earlier, the slaves built their shelters on the plantations themselves, based originally on an African model. The building materials were locally collected.

The "standard" kas di kunuku has a rectangular floor plan consisting of two rooms with a door in the middle of the front and rear of the dwelling. Symmetrically, on both sides of the door, there was a window with a wooden hatch. The kitchen stood apart from the actual home. After upright posts were placed at a regular distance from each other,

branches braided together horizontally were wrapped around the posts which served as reinforcement for further construction of the wall.

Sometimes, this braid was bound with the fibers of the sisal plant (*Agave sisalana*). Longitudinal beams were placed on top of the posts, which in turn bore the trusses with purlins. All of this was of minimal dimensions considering the negligible weight of the roof covering. The covering of the hipped roof was an approximately twenty centimeter thick layer of dried sorghum stalks which was tied directly to the purlins. Later, the corn stalk roof was often replaced by galvanized corrugated steel sheets which were much more durable. The bundled branches were completely covered with a mixture of clay, cow dung and/or blades of grass, and blended with water. Part of the kas di kunuku was given an exterior protective layer of coral or quarry stone, using the same mixture as mentioned above. Since these stacked stones were thicker on the

Kunuku house at Soto, 1977

Construction of a kunuku house

underside and tapered upwards, the kas di kunuku acquired its characteristic sloping outer walls. The inner and outer walls were plastered over with a thin layer of lime. It sometimes happened that there was no protective layer of stone and only a thin layer of lime plaster was applied to the loam. This was, of course, a cheaper method.

Because the houses with the exterior protective layer of stone have stood the test of time better, many of them are still standing today. All of the houses with only the protective lime plaster layer on the outside have disappeared.
The floor of the house was flattened before the start of construction and was made, just like the walls, from a mixture of clay and cow dung.

The kas di kunuku was built in the traditional way until around the turn of the last century. Beginning around that time, especially in the vicinity of town, many workers' houses were built of wood, the *kas di tabla*. In the first decades of the twentieth century, a new period of construction evolved with the arrival of cement and the concrete blocks.

Notes

1. Visman, 1981-1983: dl.6, 5
2. Muller, 1905 : 423 e.v
3. Visman, 1976-1977: dl.3, 20.
4. Renkema, 2016
5. Nationaal Archief, Den Haag, Inv.nr. MIKO 1237
6. Nationaal Archief, Den Haag, Inv.nr. MIKO CE 110; Ozinga, 1959: Overzichtskaart 1- B. Renkema, 2016: kaart C149
7. Nationaal Archief, Den Haag, Inv.nr. K.A. 155; Ozinga, 1959: afd.3; Renkema, 2016: kaart C157.
8. Krogt, Peter van der, 2005, 3, in Caert Thresoor, Tijdschrift voor de Geschiedenis van de Kartografie, 2005-1
9. Renkema, 1981: 16
10. Renkema, 1981: 20
11. Renkema, 1981: 151
12. Pruneti Winkel, 1987: 39
13. Renkema, 1981: 53
14. Stedman, 1799-1800: dl.3, 299
15. Ozinga, 1959: 16
16. Nationaal Archief, Den Haag. Min. v. Kol. - 3839
17. Ozinga, 1959: 30 noot 1
18. Hartog, 1961: 796
19. Amigoe, 13 juni 1885
20. Bosch, 1829: dl.1, 197
21. De Gaay Fortman, 1932-1934: 347 ; Hartog, 1961: 795
22. Klooster, 2007: 292
23. Bosch, 1836: dl. 2, 308

PLANTATION HOUSES

JEANNETTE VAN DITZHUIJZEN

01

ASCENCION

ASCENSION IS ONE OF CURAÇAO'S OLDEST ORIGINAL PLANTATIONS. IT IS NAMED AFTER THE INDIAN VILLAGE PUEBLO DE LA MADRE ASCENSION.

With its red and white shutters, country estate Ascension looms high over its surrounding greenery. The beautiful hourglass motifs on these shutters are not original since they do not appear in old drawings or paintings of Curaçao plantation houses. When, however, this estate was restored in the 1960s by the architect Serge Alexeenko, authenticity was not as strictly adhered to.

Ascension, with its important source of water, is one of Curaçao's oldest original plantations. It is named after the Indian village Pueblo de la Madre Ascension once located nearby. In 1672 Jurriaan Janszoon Exteen established the plantation with the plantation house being built not much later. The distinctive two corner towers on either side of the terrace may have been added to enhance the prestige of the owners. In any event, they offered additional storage space, and at the top there was room for the pigeons which many reasonable plantation owners kept on their property to be enjoyed as food.

Due to the nearby water source several crops could be cultivated. At the end of the seventeenth century these were *maishi chikí* (sorghum), indigo, cotton, and sugarcane. In the second half of the nineteenth century aloe was also grown.

Additionally, sheep, goats, donkeys and cows wandered the property.

The plantation owners were not always prosperous. For instance, Jonathan Ferguson, who retreated to Ascension for health reasons in 1829, was unable to properly oversee the property due to his illness. The expenses exceeded the income and, following his death in 1832, his widow was forced to sell the increasingly dilapidated plantation at a great loss.

In 1884 phosphate was discovered at "Seru Mainshi", a part of the Ascencion plantation. Following its discovery at the Tafelberg (in 1874, see Santa Barbara) people started searching for the valuable raw material in the area of several plantations. That same year the Curaçao Phosphate Company Ascencion was founded. Because the quality proved inferior to the phosphate mined at the Tafelberg the company was dissolved several years later.

The most famous inhabitant of this estate is undoubtedly Cola Debrot who would later become governor. His parents owned the estate between 1922 and 1925. He lived there for only a few months and he is said to have used the plantation house as the setting for his novella *Mijn zuster de negerin* (My Black Sister).

In 1960 the plantation, including the derelict plantation house and repositories, was sold to the Curaçao Heritage Foundation. Following an extensive renovation by the above-mentioned Alexeenko, the house was leased to the Royal Navy which opened a training facility on the site in 1965. One of the conditions of the lease was that the estate remain accessible to the public, and consequently there is a monthly Open House with music, snacks and drinks. Tourists and Curaçaoans can enjoy the views from the front and back terraces. There are also tours of the estate and its environs every Thursday.

02

BARBER

Kabrietenberg

The presbytery of Barber's church is located in the former plantation house. Almost unintentionally Father Martinus Niewindt came into possession of it.

Joseph Piñero Sillé inherited Barber in 1827 from his grandfather, the former slave Joseph Piñero, who had grown wealthy as a captain and shipowner. Beginning in 1828 Sillé rented a corn shed on his property to Niewindt who used it as a provisional church. Despite objections from the district master who believed that the presence of some 500 slaves would lead to unrest, Niewindt said mass there every week.

After Sillé's death in 1832, legal problems arose about his will and the continuation of the provisional church building. Father Niewindt then amassed 10,000 guilders and purchased the entire plantation, including the church.

In 1842 Niewindt established a Roman Catholic cemetery at Barber. When he became bishop in 1843, he founded a seminary for priests in the plantation house. After the corn barn collapsed in 1869, it was replaced by the current church in 1876.

The orchard next to the church, Hòfi Pastor, is part of Barber's parish. The oldest tree on the island, a 400-year-old kapok tree, stands there.

BEVER

Buena Vista, Corporaal

This little country house was once called Buena Vista due to its beautiful view. On the grounds are the graves of Jan Pietersz van Oxfort, his wife Johanna Mattiae and their son Thomas. Father and son were "cornets" of the cavalry at the end of the seventeenth century.

Jan Pietersz's house was so badly damaged by a hurricane in 1681 that the director of the Dutch West India Company asked him to build a new house because the old one was too close to the cavalrymen's residence. The current plantation house would therefore have been built by Pietersz, but it was most likely adapted and extended around 1800 by Jessurun Sasportas.

The house was subsequently owned by Daniel Beevers who was Surgeon-Major of the National Guard from 1828 until 1840 and the one to give the property its current name.

Somewhat later, in 1867, the house was repaired and properly restored. It had a courtyard with fruit trees and a well with clean drinking water. In the mid-twentieth century Bever was the home of Benny Maduro. By then the wells supplied only brackish water.

The house has a vestibule with a semicircular staircase that is flanked by flowerbeds. There is a set of small brick steps and a wooden garden fence between masonry columns. In 2016 there was a partial restoration.

04

BLAUW
Blije Rust, Grote Blaauw

Although Anno Blauw founded the Blauw plantation in 1700 tax documents show that there was no house built on the property until 1828. Hubertus Jacobs bought Blauw in 1917 from the pharmacist Joubert. With his Saban wife and children, Jacobs lived in the house which he personally refurbished over the years.

The family grew vegetables and owned a lot of cattle. They sold their milk, eggs, vegetables and fruit to the nuns of the Sint Elisabeth Gasthuis. In front of the house there was a *hòfi* with mango, kenepa and sapodilla trees; there were also huge mahogany trees and Mrs Jacobs grew roses. During the Second World War, Americans were stationed at Blauw. There is a museum dedicated to the war on the property.

Shell's pumping the water away from nearby Julianadorp caused the groundwater of the plantation to become salinized. That is why the family turned to stone-crushing in 1936. Pletterij Nederhorst made *blòkis* from the stones and the sand.

The family also established the beautiful Blauwbaai Beach, of which many islanders have fond memories. At times Jacobs closed the beach so that the nuns could swim undisturbed. His son, Hubert, taught them to swim.

Following the sale to Curasol in 1990, Blauw became a popular site for the construction of villas and apartments. The hotel reception and the clubhouse of the Blue Bay Golf & Beach Resort are currently located in the former plantation house. Since 2017 Blauw has had a sculpture garden of international reputation.

BLOEMHOF

Nooijt Gedagt, Porta di Heru

05

Anyone entering Bloemhof now can see why this was a very popular country retreat in previous centuries. Here, the owners who lived in the cramped city could find fresh air, serenity and space. Although the plantation supplied rainwater and grew plenty of *larahas*, the plantation house was especially important as a retreat. The laraha skins destined for the Curaçao liqueur were dried on the path leading from the Santa Rosaweg to the plantation house. This path, with its elegant *porta di heru* (wrought iron gate), was the original entrance.

The oldest preserved deed of purchase for this seven-hectare plantation dates from 1735. The plantation house itself is nineteenth-century. When Emma Lopez Penha purchased Bloemhof in 1919, the plantation had already changed hands twenty-two times.

In her book *Samen Leven*, Emma's granddaughter, May Henriquez, describes how during weekends and holidays her grandmother traveled from the Penstraat to Bloemhof in a fully loaded chauffeur-driven car, followed by a *shèrs* (horse and carriage) carrying staff and food. A special attraction for her grandchildren was the *baki*, a stone cistern filled with well water for watering the trees and plants. After it had been scrubbed and rid of algae, it was used as a swimming pool. At that time, cattle still grazed and a few times a year someone came to burn charcoal, *kima karbon*.

From the 1930s onward the plantation house was frequently rented. Emma's daughter Sarah and her son in law Joseph built a house on the grounds and called it May-Eve after their two daughters.

Unfortunately this house soon fell into disrepair and was demolished. In the 1940s a modern home was constructed for May and her husband Max. That building now houses the *Number Ten* restaurant and the Curaçao Natural History Museum.

May, a sculptor, used the coach house as a studio which can now be viewed in its original state. Whenever the plantation house was not under lease, she often organized exhibitions, theater performances and concerts there. For several years in the 1960s it was occupied by Gallery De Boog owned by May, Ben Smit and Barbara Smeets. Shortly thereafter the former cistern was converted into an office; the overflow holes and the original copper faucet are still visible.

Following the death of May Henriquez in 1999, the family decided to convert Bloemhof into a permanent cultural center. There was a thorough restoration including the adaptation of the *mangasinas* into a storage facility, archive, library, and meeting room. Since the beginning of this century the plantation house has regularly hosted cultural events and workshops as well as exhibitions of local and international artists.

In 2014 the artist Herman van Bergen used *sumpiñas*, the spines of the *wabi* (*Acacia tortuosa*), to construct the imposing Cathedral of Thorns on the foundation of May-Eve. Next to the cathedral is the outdoor studio of the sculptress Hortense Brouwn. Her sculptures and those of others are spread across the grounds.

Furthermore, there are various walking trails on the former plantation grounds. The remarkable bathhouse with its two stone baths which were once filled with water from the neighboring well via an aqueduct is hidden among the greenery. Thanks to all these renovations, the former plantation has been given a completely new purpose and is a focal point of Curaçaoan society.

| 45

Sorting the *laraha* peels, around 1940.

BLOEMPOT

Moron

06

This plantation was also called Moron after one of its oldest owners, Aron Henriquez Moron who came to Curaçao as a twenty year old in 1730. After marrying Esther Penso he went to work for his wealthy brother-in-law, Mosseh Penso. Once he became a shipowner, he went into the business of freight transport and ship insurance. In 1754 he came to own Bloempot which he most probably used as a country house for thirty years.

A century later its owner, Moses Cohen Henriquez, was able to convincingly demonstrate that the one and a half hectare small Bloempot was not a plantation. In a letter to the editor of *De Curaçaosche Courant* about the taxable value of plantations, he made it clear that Bloempot could never be compared to, for example, Klein Sint Joris. According to him, Sint Joris had the acreage for fields of sorghum, beans, and peanuts, while Bloempot barely accommodated "a quarter of a pint of corn". Moreover, the coconut and citrus trees had all perished after his purchase of Bloempot in 1833. According to the owner, Bloempot's annual yield didn't exceed 450 guilders. He himself stated that this country estate in no way deserved the designation "plantation".

Incidentally, this Cohen Henriquez was one of the protagonists in the struggle within the Jewish community on the island that, in 1864, led to the rupture and the construction of the Temple Emanu-el.

The plantation house is privately inhabited and consists of two blocks with neoclassical characteristics. At the farthest points of the front façade there are striking ornaments. The façade itself is crowned with a triangular surface (pediment), in which there is a medallion representing a flower pot with flowers. Empty flower pots adorn the pillars of the entrance gate to the far left of the plantation house. The large cistern to the right of the house has a beautiful saddle roof.

BONA VISTA
Vriendenwijck

The estate now known as Bona Vista, likely called Buena Vista originally, was given the lovely name of Vriendenwijck (Friends Quarter) in the eighteenth century. The new name didn't stick and soon it was again called Bona Vista. The name makes sense since from its vantage point upon a hill one could see seventeen surrounding estates.

The plantation had many owners. Between 1787 and 1857 there were seventeen of them, including a former slave, Maria Loenen, who inherited the plantation in 1850 from Casper Hensle. At the end of the eighteenth century, construction of a small plantation house, consisting of the main body of the house, a corridor, and two wings, was initiated. The thicker walls are evidence that this is the oldest part of the plantation house.

The estate's inventory of 1834 includes building supplies such as roofing and paving materials. In that same year a new section was added. This addition is now the entrance. The entrance is thus located in the original rear of the building. The new ornate façade probably dates to a later period around the end of the nineteenth century. To either side of the main entrance two corner structures were added in the mid-twentieth century. Noteworthy of this structure is that almost all of the walls were built with yellow bricks rather than crushed stones and coral. This can be seen in two places in the interior. Originally the kitchen was detached from the main house. During the restoration of 2002 the covered corridor connecting the two buildings was converted into a passageway.

Although the owner Matthias Lulls had a storehouse built at the end of the eighteenth century, the plantation did not yield much. All fruit and vegetables grown on the plantation were reserved for personal consumption. A 1799 sales agreement indicates that there was also cattle. Mention is made of "the right of 60 sheep and two cows to graze in its meadows". The sale of drinking water from an underground well provided an important source of revenue. The water was transported to town by donkey. Due to its proximity to town the plantation was used mainly as a country retreat.

Bona Vista's importance as a water plantation became obvious with its purchase by the government in 1923. The water from the plantation was sold in town and to ships that used it in their steam boilers.

In 2002 the country house was restored into a boutique hotel under the direction of architect Henk Bolivar. These days a couple runs this charming bed and breakfast with newly built apartments surrounding a swimming pool. The nineteenth-century coach house and horse stable contain three apartments. Bona Vista is now, just as in the nineteenth century, a place to escape the hustle and bustle of the city.

BONAM

Bonnam, Fortuna, 't Fortuyn

The 't Fortuyn plantation was already in existence in 1743. It received its current name after Joseph Bonan purchased the plantation in 1747.

At the end of the nineteenth century Bonam was praised as 'very rich in water and forest lands' and 'enjoying the privilege of keeping a large number of cattle'.

In the early twentieth century, cows, goats, sheep and chickens were still wandering on the plantation. Clara Curiel was the owner then. The next owner, Alexander "Chang" Bloem, lived there with his children and grandchildren for over 25 years.. Because the three bedrooms didn't provide sufficient space, he built an apartment for his sons. Behind the house, his wife Maria had a flower garden that included roses and tuberoses which she sold to a flower shop in Punda. In the adjoining orchard there were medlar, mango and tamarind trees.

After Chang's death in 1942, the plantation came to be owned by the government which then sold the traditionally built and partially restored plantation house, including the annexes, wells, mills and trees, to Domingos Rodrigues Conduto in 1957.

Conduto lived there with his family and for an extended period of time had a large vegetable garden and fruit trees. He also kept chickens, pigs, cows and goats. He sold the meat and eggs. Later the plantation house grew dilapidated. The house still belongs to the family.

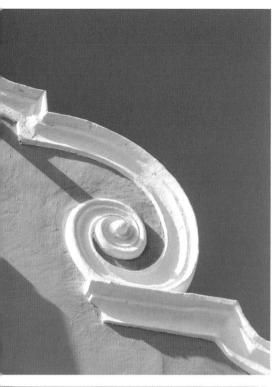

BRAKKEPUT ABOU

This plantation house with a panoramic view of Spaanse Water originates in the eighteenth century with later additions, such as the entrance with triangular façade, dating from the year 1877. The baroque bell façade, which opens into a spiral curl (volute), dates from 1795. The other side of the plantation house has a "more modern" gable.

The 1,500 rubber trees planted at Brakkeput Abou in 1907 did not survive, nor did the bananas that failed due to lack of care. In 1908, a new planting took place at the bidding of Antonius Dittmar, who had come to Curaçao as a soldier. Four years later he died in the plantation house.

In the 1970s, Herman Verboom rented the plantation house from Margot van Henneigen, who was better known as *Margot di Brakapoti*. Verboom's *Grafisch Ontwerp Buro (Graphic Design Office)* was based there. The house had heretofore been empty for years because it was said to be haunted. Keys were therefore unnecessary then.

In the meantime the house has been beautifully restored by the architectural firm *Studio Acht* and is privately occupied. Around a section of the house there is a modern covered terrace.

BRAKKEPUT ARIBA

Nooitgedagt

At one point in the past Brakkeput used to be one plantation, but it was later divided into Lower (Abou), Middle (Meimei) and Upper (Ariba).

Brakkeput Ariba is best known for the Huize Don Bosco work camp for unemployed boys aged twelve to twenty which the Crusaders of Saint John established in 1937. The plantation house was purchased for this purpose by the Apostolic Vicariate. Initially the intention was to provide the boys with training in agriculture on the plantation. Some of the boys, however, wanted a vocational education and thus, rather than being only a boarding school for boys from Bándabou, there was also a trade school on site. When an outbuilding became available on the terrain in 1962, the *Stichting Vakantieoorden* (Foundation for Holiday Destinations) of the White Yellow Cross was established there.

Incidentally, the merchant David Raphael (its owner from 1792 to 1807) once granted the plantation and forty slaves to Martha Sambo for "faithful and loyal services for a long series of years". As long as he lived she was not allowed to sell the plantation and had to give him 900 pesos a year. After his death in 1813, she sold Brakkeput Ariba to Salomon Salom Delvalle.

Once the SBO-school Maris Stella vacated the plantation house, it was renovated. It has been empty for years now.

BRAKKEPUT MEIMEI

Klijne Bracke Putt

This plantation was a diversified farm with animal husbandry and the cultivation of sorghum and beans. The fruit and dairy were sold in town and to the ships in the harbor.

Shell purchased the plantation and the plantation house in 1929. In 1938 the Salvation Army established a youth home there similar to the Roman Catholic home at Brakkeput Ariba, and that existed there until 1945.

Later the plantation house served as part of the Asiento Sports and Recreation Association for Shell employees, and was used, for example, "for picnics in the courtyards behind the plantation house". There were also wooden stilted weekend homes. Additionally, the plantation house was rented out for a variety of receptions, parties, and barbecues. Thus, in September 1965, then Queen Juliana and Prince Bernhard were guests at a luncheon hosted there by the Island Territory.

After Shell left in 1985 and following a major refurbishment, the plantation house was acquired by the Curaçao Heritage Foundation. The house was rented out to The Trader Party Service which continued to use the plantation house for receptions and parties. After another renovation, the popular Brakkeput Mei Mei restaurant has occupied the plantation house since 1999. Later, an open-air terrace with a stage was added for concerts and events. The fact that what is currently the rear of the house was originally the official entrance is evidenced by the beautiful, expansive staircase leading to the patio of the U-shaped plantation house.

BRIEVENGAT

De Hoop

Cornelis Janszoon Sprock from The Hague had only just moved to Curaçao in 1847 when he bought the then dilapidated Brievengat. He cultivated new pastures, repaired the buildings, and built new structures.

In the twentieth century, neglect followed again when Shell bought the plantation for the water it needed for its refining process. Later Brievengat appeared to have no water at all, but by then the purchase had already been completed. This was a death sentence for the large plantation house that dated to circa 1750. In the early 1950s Shell decided to demolish the house which had fallen into ruin. Some Curaçaoans initiated a rescue operation under the leadership of Percy Cohen Henriquez. They founded the Curaçao Heritage Foundation in 1954 and bought the plantation house from Shell for one guilder. In 1955, with a donation of 75,000 guilders from the industrialist Bernard van Leer of Van Leer's Vatenfabriek, the house was restored to its former glory by the architect Serge Alexeenko

Later that century, René Hoetjes turned Brievengat into a popular recreation center which holds good memories for many Curaçaoans. There was Indonesian *rijsttafel* every Friday evening, followed by dancing on the terrace to live music provided by *The Happy Peanuts*. During the day tourists visiting the island from cruise ships could enjoy performances of folk dances in and around the beautifully restored plantation house. By 2012 the dances were over. Thereafter the plantation house served a variety of functions but it is, at present, unoccupied.

CAS ABOU

Engelenberg

The Cas Abou plantation is a merging of the Engelenberg and Giftenberg plantations. Willebrord van Engelen, then the interim director of the Dutch West India Company, established Engelenburg in 1686 and built a house there.

August Statius Muller owned both Engelenberg and Giftenberg and, in 1838, combined them. Following the unification, according to Machiel Visman, Giftenberg's house was called e *kas abou* (the house yonder). That term later came to refer to the house of the merged plantation Engelenberg, and thus the seventeenth century plantation house came to possess its current name: Cas Abou.

The house fell into ruin until the 1960s when it was completely restored under the guidance of the architect Serge Alexeenko. Remarkably, located downwind at the western side of the structure, there is an outhouse that can accommodate two people. There are also a coach house and the ruins of a *mangasina*.

In 1980 the plantation fell into the hands of a developer wishing to restore the plantation. His plans never materialized, and in 1991 the *Ambtenaren Pensioenfonds Nederlandse Antillen* (Civil Servants Pension Fund for the Netherlands Antilles) took over the plantation. Two years later, a small hotel with a restaurant opened its doors in the plantation house, but it soon closed. The completely refurbished Cas Abou beach has been open to the public ever since, and it is one of the most popular beaches on the island.

The plantation house is still empty but there are plans for a new restoration and repurposing.

CAS CORA
Vredenberg

14

**IN 2014, THE FORMER PLANTATION AGAIN
BECAME A FARM GROWING ORGANIC
VEGETABLES.**

**In February 1844 Cornelis Janszoon Sprock arrived from
The Hague to start trading in Curaçao. Two months
later, he, along with Jean Pierre Cornets de Groot van
Kraaijenburg, bought the small plantation Vredenberg,
now better known as Cas Cora. Until 1863 Janszoon Sprock
was district master of the third district. Incidentally, a
later owner, J.A. Penso, named the plantation Penso's Park
in 1892.**

| 69

Sprock sailed to Curaçao on the same ship as the returning
governor Van Raders, the initiator of the cochineal
cultivation. While still in in the Netherlands they had
agreed that Sprock would grow nopal cacti in Curaçao.
Sprock kept his word and at Cas Cora planted nopal cacti
for the cultivation of the cochineal lice that were the
source of the carmine red dye.

There were a lot of cattle on the plantation and Janszoon
Sprock grew the usual crops, such as *maishi chikí*
(sorghum). This Sprock was also owner of Brievengat and
after the medical officer, G.A.L. Ferguson, bought Cas Cora
in 1865, the two gentlemen entered into a contentious
relationship. Ferguson accused Sprock of allowing the
cattle of Brievengat to roam uncontrollably, so that
dozens of cows would devour the Para grass carefully
cultivated by Ferguson at Cas Cora.

Mid-twentieth century cattle still grazed at Cas Cora: it was then a farm, operated by the Adriaanse and Ten Broeke families, with approximately a hundred cows and sorghum crops that fed the cows. In the old *mangasinas* to the left of the mansion, they processed their own milk into pasteurized milk, yogurt, cream and chocolate milk, while other plantations, such as Klein and Groot Sint Joris and Santa Cruz, also brought their milk to Cas Cora for pasteurization.

In 2014, the former plantation again became a farm growing organic vegetables. Due to the presence of dams there is sufficient water and the soil has steadily improved over the centuries. Enthusiastic young owners opened the restaurant Hòfi Cas Cora in one of the plantation's newer buildings.

The plantation house itself is rather neglected and was once unattractively renovated. The shutters that closed the front gallery were replaced by sliding windows, and modern floor tiles have been laid over cement tiles. Originally the house most probably had wooden flooring. The semicircular staircase made of yellow bricks at the front of the entrance is still almost intact. The current owners intend to restore the other buildings in the future, but these restorations will probably take some time.

15 | CERITO
De Vrede

Seritu means "little hill" and that might be the origin of this plantation's name. Although sales advertisements regularly referred to it as a plantation, it is questionable whether it actually was.

An ad from 1852, for example, states: "This plantation features an extensive piece of very fertile land and slave houses". So too, in 1877, when the house was for rent by its owner, D.A. Jesurun, he described a plantation, complete with "a cistern, a well, a bathing spot, a carriage house, and proper amenities for a family". Nonetheless, at the end of the century, measurements made it apparent that the terrain was no larger than 1400 m2.

The classicist house, with columns supporting a pediment, was probably built in the second half of the nineteenth century. Plantation land might have been sold and this house subsequently used as a country retreat. For example, a photograph dating to 1898, shows the family of Haim Da Costa Gomez at Cerito, which the caption states was a country retreat at the time.

During the early war years the poet Frits van der Molen, co-founder of the literary magazine De Stoep, lived in Cerito. Later, the Pietersz family lived here until the beginning of this century. Since 2010 it has been owned by Orco Bank which had it thoroughly renovated. The bank's offices are located in a contemporary addition to the rear of the plantation house.

CHOBOLOBO

Chobolobo is one of the gardens and plantations surrounding a former salt pan to the southeast of the Schottegat. Whether salt was actually harvested here is unclear, but the location explains why Chobolobo was previously named De Zoutpan (the Salt Pan). The name Chobolobo is probably a distortion of Sebollobo, the name that was used in 1796, when the free mulatta Anna Matthew was its owner. She might have been an Indian.

Chobolobo is not really a plantation but rather more of a garden. Probably built as a country retreat around 1800, the author Teenstra mentions the two-story plantation house in his1836 writings.

Today the plantation house is best known as the center of the Curaçao liqueur made from the peels of the orange apple, the *laraha*. At the end of the nineteenth century, several Curaçaoan entrepreneurs, including pharmacists Isaac Chumaceiro and Edgar Senior, made orange liqueur. Using a recipe belonging to Chumaceiro's grandfather, they started distilling Curaçao liqueur behind their Botica Excelsior on the Heerenstraat. The peels of the laraha came primarily from the Senior family plantation at Klein Kwartier. At the time, the pharmacists also exported small quantities of the liqueur to the United States. The distillery was later moved to the Zonstraat in Punda.

In 1947 Chumaceiro's widow, who still owned the family recipe, was bought out, and Senior & Co continued the large-scale production of the well-known Curaçao liqueur. In the same year, Senior & Co purchased the Chobolobo plantation house.

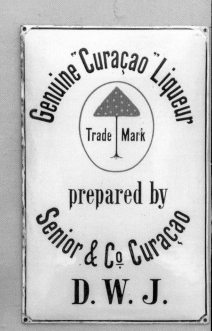

The production and storage of the liqueur continues to take place in the old *mangasinas* of the plantation house. Since the early 1960s, Alcolado Glacial, which is indispensable as a proven remedy for all kinds of ailments, has also been produced there and is exported worldwide. The copper distillation kettle that dates to 1896 is still in use.

After its purchase in 1947, the plantation house was renovated under the supervision of the architect Johan Heinrich Werner. The original purpose was the organization of tastings and the establishment of a reception area for visitors to the liqueur distillery. At the time, however, that venture was unprofitable so in 1949 a nightclub was opened for music and dancing under the stars on the outside terrace.

Today, Chobolobo receives large busloads of tourists who come for tours and tastings many times a day. The unique bottles are especially popular as collectors' items. The peels from which the liqueur is distilled still come from Curaçao.

During a restoration of the plantation house in 2014, the old storehouses were repurposed as a museum and information center. The staff canteen was housed in one of the old servants' quarters. A year later, architect Anko van der Woude designed a café with a modern roof spanning the outdoor terrace, making the café appear as if it is floating above the plantation house which it sits behind. So here too, just as is the case with some other plantation houses, a perfect convergence of old and new has been accomplished.

DANIEL
Malpais

Due to the poorer quality of its soil, Daniel was initially called Malpais (bad land). But the first name of Daniel Ellis, the founder of the plantation at the beginning of the eighteenth century, has certainly persisted. It is thought that he bought the land from the government in 1711.

In the nineteenth century, two former slaves, one after another, became the owners of Daniel. First, Lourens Serni, freed in 1850, bought the Daniel plantation in 1867 and remained its owner for at least twenty years. In 1873 he owned about 800 goats and sheep and around forty cows. A year earlier, Serni had purchased the Grote Berg plantation. Serni was a butcher by trade and, along with C. Maduro, he advertised in newspapers "the best meat" for sale. In 1884, with Serni's permission and for a fee of six guilders per month, a police station was placed on the Daniel plantation.

The second former slave who came to own Daniel was landowner Adolph van Uytrecht. He was one of two sons his father, Willem van Uytrecht, sired with his slave, Françoise Serafina de Condé, and thus Adolph was born into slavery in 1858. His father Willem died in 1893, and a year later Adolph bought the Daniel plantation with his inheritance. After his

death in 1902, Adolph was buried on the plantation, but earlier in this century his grave was destroyed by bulldozers.

The contractor H.J.M. van Lieshout bought the plantation house in 1976. At that time it was practically a ruin with only the walls still standing. Van Lieshout restored Daniel to its original state and furnished it with antique Curaçao furniture. In 1983 he offered the house for sale. It was then briefly owned by the Dutch television director Jef Rademakers, who leased it to an individual who ran the plantation house as a hotel and diving center. Since 1997 it has been owned by Jan Francke.

After purchasing the house, Francke immediately had a large covered terrace added to its front, thereby hiding the two dormer windows from view. A few months later, the plantation house was declared a protected monument. Nowadays Francke has, in addition to a restaurant, a gallery in the plantation house where his works and that of local artists can be seen.

The seventeenth century house is one of Curaçao's older plantation houses. Via an aqueduct the rainwater is drained to a cistern with a steep gable roof. The ruins of a *mangasina* still stand at the left side of the plantation house.

DE GOEDE HOOP

Popo

18

De Goede Hoop plantation house or Popo is beautifully situated on a hill and consists of a core with four galleries all around. The roof of the large, pillared front terrace was added in the twentieth century.

The house most likely dates prior to 1800. We are certain that when the property was sold in 1776 it included a residence, a warehouse and a dovecote. Serving primarily as a country retreat, it enjoyed "the right to use public land for 50 sheep to graze on".

It is noteworthy that the current inhabitant is a direct descendant of the man who bought the estate in 1807: Bernardus Anthony Cancrijn. Apparently, he purchased the estate as an investment, a common practice at the time. He personally lived in the Van den Brandhofstraat in Scharloo. Upon acquiring the property he immediately took over part of the inventory, namely, one negro, one donkey cart, two mares, two donkeys, and an assortment of gardening tools.

Mondecir Martinus Ecker, who had been born into slavery, became its new owner in the mid-nineteenth century. He was married to Dorothea Hipolita Leon, an illegitimate but legally recognized daughter of Anton Leon, the grandfather of its current inhabitant. The Goede Hoop was subsequently sold to Anton Leon's son Bernardus. According to the deed the plantation had by then "declined into a poor state of repair".

Bernardus Leon rented out the plantation house until his son Sergio Leon and his American wife returned to Curaçao in 1962 to open a gynecology practice. The couple moved to De Goede Hoop to fulfill a wish that Sergio Leon had cherished since his early childhood. From the beginning he has properly maintained the plantation house and its surrounding grounds. It is furnished with countless antique pieces, many of which were personally restored by Leon. As a modern addition, he built a swimming pool halfway up the hill.

DE HOOP

19

Merchant Matthias Beck built this nineteenth century De Hoop and used it as a weekend retreat. The house is said to have burned down after which it was rebuilt using mostly wood for the interior and exterior walls. The foundation, the round water basin on the left and a second water basin are still made of raw quarry stone.

The Canadian officer Ray, who remained on the island after the war due to his marriage to a local woman, transformed De Hoop into a true fairytale castle. This was achieved by adding a tower roof onto the water basin to the left of the house, and to the right of the house a castle tower was built to accommodate a bathroom. A real castle gate was erected in front of the entrance and battlements were installed above the gutters. A subsequent owner painted the house pink and organized childrens' parties there. This led to De Hoop being called the "pink castle".

In 2005 the current owner stripped De Hoop of these additions and painted it blue. The original round water basin has been retained and a part of the castle gate is still visible at the entrance. The light blue house therefore looks like a Curaçaoan plantation house once again. In the garden vegetables are grown among the age-old *kenepa's*, *shimaruku's*, tamarind trees and *apeldams*, and De Hoop itself is available for rent.

The plantation house is often incorrectly referred to as Toni Kunchi, but that house was demolished in 1965 to make way for the construction of the Toni Kunchi district.

20

DOKTERSTUIN

Klein Ascencion, Plantage Docter

From 1976 until the end of the 1980s the government doctor practiced in this two-story residence, but the name Dokterstuin (Doctor's Garden) has existed much longer. The name appears to date back to one of the earliest owners, the physician Jan Bernagie who was given the plantation by his brother Bastiaan toward the end of the seventeenth century. So in those days it was the doctor's garden.

In the mid-nineteenth century Hendrik de Quartel sold the Dokterstuin and Pannekoek plantations to the government. Beginning in 1863 Pannekoek became the residence of Jan Jacob Van Dam, the district supervisor of the fifth district. According to Van Dam, Dokterstuin was so dilapidated it didn't merit restoration. In any event, one year later, in 1864, all of its roofing tiles were removed and taken to Pannekoek. Only a police station, where the military police checked bills of lading necessary for fifth district residents transporting their agricultural products into town, remained at Dokterstuin.

When, in 1871, the district supervisor had to acquire his own residence, the government sold Dokterstuin (and Pannekoek) to Willem Simon ("shon Wilmu") da Costa Gomez. Apparently there was hardly anything left of the original Dokterstuin because shon Wilmu had the current house built and moved into it circa 1880.

At the beginning of the twentieth century the government reconsidered its earlier decision and the district supervisor was again granted an official residence. At first this was Siberie until the government was able to buy back Dokterstuin from shon Wilmu in 1913. The estate was restored and the district supervisor took up residence there. The best known and last district supervisor was Johan Marin Statius van Eps who left in 1953.

For some time the district office at Dokterstuin then served as an auxiliary office for administrative affairs and as a polling station at elections. Between 1968 and 1974 the building accommodated a school but the ramshackle condition of the house necessitated its closing. After another restoration the government doctor, J.H. Arendzen, established his practice in the plantation house.

In the early 1990s, just as in 1863, the roof collapsed and again the house fell into decay. In 1995 Mama Bebi was allowed to rent the property from the government on condition that she restore it at her own expense. The entire family helped with the restoration,and since its renovation Bebi's daughter runs a typical Curaçaoan restaurant on the premises. The space occupied by the kitchen in district supervisor Van Eps' time is now the bar and the main living area is furnished with antique Curaçaoan furniture. The attic that occupied the space above the living room has, however, been removed. Guests can now enjoy a creole lunch outside in the shade exactly in the spot where the district supervisor's chickens used to enjoy free range.

GAITO
Vreeland, Gaitu

For a century, beginning in 1783, this plantation was in the same hands as Groot Kwartier. In 1830, however, Martha Elisabeth Lamont, owner of both plantations, preferred to live in Gaito rather than in Groot Kwartier. The question is whether she lived in the same house as the one that is currently there.

Given the 1758 map drawn by Jan Esdré, the son of the owner then, there was a different house there at the time. Of note are the dovecote, the *mangasina* with a threshing floor, a grain shed and the slave houses that Esdre recorded on paper.

According to Teenstra, who passed the house circa 1832, Gaito was then a rather insignificant "garden". In the mid-twentieth century, however, Gaito was a cattle farm, as evidenced by a photograph of cows walking behind the elegant plantation house. A beautiful ornamental garden was laid out in front of the house.

The purportedly nineteenth century plantation house has modest curls in its façade and stylized floral decorations above its windows. In the twentieth century the stately entrance, consisting of pillars and a large balcony, was added. At the rear, a slightly smaller balcony is supported by two pillars. Gaito has been beautifully restored by its current owner, the Advent Missionary Society.

According to Father Brenneker there used to be a water reservoir in front of the house with a weathercock or *gaíto*, which clearly explains the property's name.

GIROUETTE
Rijkenberg

In 1828, due to large debts, Jeosuah de Sola offered to sell seven houses and two plantations, including Girouette. Several months later, because there was hardly any interest, he organized a lottery with three houses and Girouette as prizes. Again he met with no success.

In exasperation he dismissed the lottery because, he claimed, "the majority of the people of present day Curaçao are reluctant to do a favor and their affection does not extend to lending a helping hand to a man in need".

| 93

At a forced auction in 1830 Girouette again failed to sell. Only after De Sola's death in 1832 did a new owner purchase Girouette for much less than its estimated value.

The plantation was founded around 1700 by Dirk Rijken, hence the name Rijkenberg. Girouette is a distortion of the name of its eighteenth-century owner, Jean Pierre Sorhouet.

A striking detail at the rear of the plantation house is a funnel-shaped extension: through this a workhand could pour water from outside for the bath inside the house.

In 1972 the eighteenth century Girouette was drastically restored by architect Serge Alexeenko.

GRANBEEUW
St. Jansberg, Seru Bientu

It is hard to imagine now, but according to the 1911 Werbata map this house once stood among wells, windmills, dams and an orchard. It is, unfortunately, unknown what exactly grew on the small plantation and whether or not a lot of cattle grazed on the land.

According to Father Brenneker, around 1858 the plantation was owned by a certain S. Granbeeuw. The kitchen was at one time converted into a bathroom, initially retaining the baking oven, but unfortunately it has disappeared over the course of the last ten years.

In the twentieth century, between 1932 and 1947, Nicolaas Herman Henriquez lived there. He was married to Virginia Elsevijf, the daughter of the former slave Herman Elsevijf who had worked his way up as an architect and landowner after his manumission.

Granbeeuw then had various residents, such as the well-known artists' family De Rooy in the early 1960s. Later, Van den Brink's poultry farm settled in and around the plantation house. In the 1990s, the Zorg en Hoop retirement home took occupancy of the house.

Following a major restoration under Tom Massizo and Kees Tukker, Granbeeuw became a multifunctional recreational center. Later on Restaurant Peppers started a catering training center there as part of a second chance education project led by Louis Berendsen. At the end of 2018, the Colombian businessman Montana bought the plantation house. He will continue the catering activities. The Montana beer brewery is located in the annex.

GROOT DAVELAAR

Daflá , Welgelegen

This plantation house immediately stands out due to its unique, octagonal shape. It was built by Antoine Martis around 1873 on behalf of its owner at the time, Juan Ricardo Blanch, a Venezuelan refugee. The house features neoclassical characteristics combined with the local architectural style.

While traveling in Europe, Blanch gathered ideas for this house with its double stairs leading to a terrace. Surrounding the octagonal sala were the sleeping quarters that were, in turn, enclosed by a circular gallery. On the second floor there was also a sala with French doors and shuttered windows. From here the residents enjoyed a view overlooking the many neighboring plantation houses. The bathroom, with its wooden bath and toilet stool, was positioned above the water reservoir. The basement was intended for the servants.

Cornelis van Groot Davelaar established the plantation in 1732, but it eventually fell into the hands of Moses Abraham Jesurun in 1828. This merchant lived in the city, but spent his weekends on his plantation which was located close to water sufficient for the cultivation of fruit and vegetables and the catering of cattle. Additionally, lime was burned there. From his plantation Jesurun could easily supply his ship, the *Enterprise*, with water, vegetables, and fruit.

In 1836, after several years of drought and crop failures, Jesurun left for Caracas with his family, and the plantation was sold to Samuel Cohen Henriquez, a descendant of one of the richest families in Curaçao. He was not successful either: in 1840 almost all palm trees on the island succumbed to a plague of scale lice, and there followed several extremely dry years. He sold the plantation but adversity persisted. Salinization of the wells led to disappointing crops and, after a forced auction, the neglected plantation with its poorly maintained plantation house was bought by the above-mentioned Blanch in 1870.

Financial difficulties due to the Venezuelan trade blockades, forced Blanch to resell his newly built house and plantation in 1877. In subsequent years the house changed hands regularly. For example, the firm of C. Winkel & Co owned Groot Davelaar from 1906 to 1932. It used the cool plantation house for the storage of foodstuffs, among other things. In the warm summer months the family dwelt there. Just like the other houses belonging to the Winkel family, Groot Davelaar was painted red.

The plantation house then received various tenants and sub-tenants. In the 1960's, for example, the tile manufacturer Mosaicos Sanchez was located in the basement. Mosaicos Sanchez produced the famous Curaçao cement tiles.

After a restoration, restaurant De Taveerne opened its doors in Groot Davelaar in 1978. In 1996, after the house had been empty for some time and the weeds within grew rampant, it was again in urgent need of restoration. After this last renovation it was, along with Zeelandia and Vredenberg, the first plantation house designated a protected monument by the island territory.

Groot Davelaar continued to function as a restaurant for only a short time. In 2003, it was occupied by the Zeelandia Opleidingen Groep, now known as the University of the Dutch Caribbean.

GROOT
KWARTIER
Rustenburgh

IN FRONT OF THE PLANTATION HOUSE, WHICH USED TO PRACTICALLY BORDER THE SCHOTTEGAT, CANNONS FOUND IN THE IMMEDIATE VICINITY ARE A REMINDER OF MANUEL PIAR WHO, IN 1804, HELPED DRIVE THE ENGLISH OFF THE ISLAND.

This plantation house originally had a U-shaped floor plan with a patio, but it was later enclosed. According to Teenstra in 1832 the front was supported "at its Eastern end by ten beautiful pillars". These pillars are part of a gallery that is open on the ground floor and closed on the floor above.

According to an old transport deed of 1783, Martha Elisabeth Lamont received the plantation, along with the building, from her stepfather Casper Lodewijk van Uytrecht. It is certain that she herself rented out the plantation house in 1830 and lived on the Gaito plantation. Her second husband, Benjamin Philips, and others were buried at Groot Kwartier, but the cemetery has disappeared. In front of the plantation house, which used to practically border the Schottegat, cannons found in the immediate vicinity are a reminder of Manuel Piar who, in 1804, helped drive the English off the island.

For more than a century, from 1863 to 1964, the Jesurun family owned Groot Kwartier. In 1888, Abraham Benjamin Jesurun was one of the first planters on the island to build windmills that could irrigate the 400 banana, *laraha* and divi divi trees. Numerous cattle were also provided with

water in this way. In addition, Groot Kwartier was an important water supplier. Its well water was brought to town or to the ships in the harbor with water pontoons. There were salt pans in the Schottegat.

After Shell bought portions of the plantation for employee housing and the recreational center Rust and Burgh, Frans Vreugdenhil bought the plantation house and the rest of the plantation in 1964. It was important to him that the plantation house not be demolished, and he restored the building entirely at his own expense. He later received a plaque from Monumentenzorg Curaçao (Curaçao Heritage Foundation). His son and daughter-in-law lived there for a short while, after which the house was leased to the Venezuelan consul. At the time it was called Casa Venezuela.

From 1987 on an insurance company occupied the plantation house, but at the beginning of this century it was empty and the house became rather dilapidated. Following its restoration in 2010 by owner Rick Baljet, where the interior renovation and the choice of colors were overseen by the architect Cees den Heijer, the trust office, Trustmoore, rented the plantation house.

Except for the unusual gray color, from the outside the plantation house now looks as it did in the past. Inside it radiates a modern office environment, and the monumental staircase at the entrance, designed by Den Heijer, immediately catches one's eye. The interior of the old cistern is painted blue and serves as a workspace for the IT department. The original yellow bricks still lie outside and on the covered patio. The plantation house thus presents a fine combination of old and new.

Under the supervision of Den Heijer, a modern building in the style of the Rooi Catootje library was erected to the right in front of the mansion over the course of 2019.

26

GROOT PISCADERA

The Groot Piscadera plantation belonged to the West India Company. Here, around 1700, many slaves worked at raising cattle and the harvesting of beans, sorghum, divi divi pods and cane sugar.

In 1831 the owner, Martinus Bernardus Schotborgh, complained about the many people who, without authorization, used the road that passed through his plantation and Klein Piscadera. "The Noble Lord Director of this island" announced in the newspaper that - under penalty of a stiff fine – this had to end. In 1834 Schotborgh sold the plantation and then bought Ascencion.

At the end of the nineteenth century Charles August Jones became the owner of the now heavily dilapidated Groot Piscadera. Jones installed fencing, dug wells, placed windmills and provided proper fertilization. He planted new trees in the courtyards. Professor Went, who, in 1901, reviewed the agricultural situation in Curaçao, cited Groot Piscadera as an example for other plantations.

In 1928, Shell purchased Piscadera as a source of water and for the construction of company housing for Shell staff. Thirty years later Christiaan van der Mark had a farm there; he and his family lived in the plantation house.

Around 1980, the contractor Theo van Bergen restored the plantation house that dates from the early nineteenth century. Since 1999 it has been the property of Bea and Willem Moedt who replaced the old shutter windows with window frames.

27

GROOT SANTA MARTHA

Groot Sint Marten

This plantation was probably founded between 1670 and 1690, and the plantation house dates from that time as well. The large gate that encloses the patio, on the other hand, is from the twentieth century. An image of Saint Martha has been incorporated into the pediment.

Traditionally the plantation was an important salt plantation, certainly after David Dovale installed new salt pans in the bay of Santa Martha in the first half of the nineteenth century.

Gerard Henri van der Linde Schotborgh, as of 1914 a co-owner and a planter through and through, lived in the manor house. In 1933 financial difficulties forced him to sell Groot Santa Martha to Jan Ernst van der Dijs, who also went on to live in the plantation house. Groot Santa Martha became an important cattle plantation whose milk, cheese, butter, and beef were sold in town. The orchard supplied sufficient fruit and, among other crops, sorghum was cultivated for personal consumption.

When its revenues did not justify its expenses, the plantation was sold to the government in 1952. Following the restoration of the plantation house and *mangasinas* in the early 1970s, a workshop for the physically or mentally handicapped, *Tayer Sosial Santa Martha*, gradually occupied the plantation with its many annexes. Souvenirs, including goatskin tanned on site, are made there. Furniture is also repaired. The plantation house itself is partially furnished as a museum.

28

GROOT SINT JORIS

Chinchó

This country house has a striking, semi-circular façade with a palmette decoration. Below the façade a marble slab dating to the eighteenth century depicts a harp-playing King David and the text *Beautiful View*. This slab was most likely added by one of the former Jewish owners.

Groot Sint Joris has been inhabited by the Perret Gentil family for over 130 years. Casper Perret Gentil bought the plantation in 1884. His son Federico, the grandfather of the current occupant, assumed ownership in 1921. Five years later he sold the plantation to Shell which extracted water from the grounds for its refining process. The family subsequently rented the house and part of the land from Shell. Until 1962 that land was used for agriculture and cattle breeding. On the plantation there were many *laraha* trees, the peels of which were dried on the square in front of the plantation house and sold to the liquer factory on Chobolobo.

After the departure of Shell in 1985, the house became the property of the Island Territory of Curaçao. Although the façade still looks attractive, the house is no longer habitable due to lack of maintenance. The family, however, still lives in one of the annexes. The view of Sint Jorisbaai from the back terrace is impressive, and in clear weather you can see Bonaire.

GROOT SINT MICHIEL

Although the name Groot (Large) Sint Michiel would suggest otherwise, the plantation house is smaller than the one at Klein (Little) Sint Michiel. The term "groot" happens to refer only to the size of the plantation. The current plantation house seems to have been built atop the remains of the original one at the beginning of the nineteenth century.

The Henriquez family owned Groot Sint Michiel from 1786 until the plantation was auctioned off, at the request of a number of trading companies, in 1874. The house then was the property of the merchant Mordechay Jeosuah Henriquez and his wife Leah who resided in Venezuela. According to the advertisement of sale, there were a house and other buildings on the plantation grounds. Whether the heavily mortgaged plantation, "with the right to herd sheep and goats, and possessing other cattle corals", could still be profitable could not be "estimated with accuracy", according to the ad.

The Venezuelan Santos Vincente Gomez acquired the plantation in the 1930s and sold it to Shell during the war years. The company built Julianadorp on the plantation grounds. Water was also extracted from the ground. From 1948 to 1976 the Dutch farmer Jan Brouwer had a dairy farm on the remaining grounds of the plantation. Joe Pinedoe then established the Rancho Alegre riding school there. The plantation house has belonged to the government since the departure of Shell in 1985.

30 GROTE BERG

Seru Grandi

What is most striking about this large, two-story block-shaped house is its hipped roof and three dormer windows in the form of a pediment. One can hardly imagine that in the past there were many goats and sheep roaming around this plantation house.

Just as was the case with Daniel, this plantation was twice owned by former slaves. Lourens Serni, born a slave, bought Daniel in 1867 and then bought Grote Berg five years later. Prior to the abolition of slavery in 1863, he himself had purchased three slaves, one of whom was his sister.

Another owner and former slave was Leonard van Uytrecht, Adolph van Uytrecht's brother who bought Daniel. Just like Adolph, he used the inheritance from his father, Willem van Uytrecht, for the purchase of a plantation in 1895. Their mother was Françoise Serafina de Condé, a slave at Santa Cruz, which was then owned by Willem van Uytrecht. Leonard and his descendants lived in the plantation house until the middle of the twentieth century.

At the end of the last century, notary Elco Rosario owned Grote Berg. The plantation house has now been vacant and neglected, but there are plans to restore it to its former glory.

HABAAI
Welgelegen

Beginning in 1651, Sephardic Jews from Amsterdam and Brazil settled in Curaçao. The Dutch West India Company granted them a plot of land north of the Schottegat and soon several plantations such as De Hoop, Bleinheim, Marchena, and Welgelegen appeared. This area of Curaçao was therefore called the Jewish Quarter until well into the nineteenth century.

In the eighteenth century the Welgelegen plantation was named Habaai, presumably a distortion of the Gabay Henriquez surname, the family which had owned the plantation since 1771. There they had a diversified farm with both livestock and agriculture. The baroque plantation house with elegant façades dating from the mid-eighteenth century was likely already there. The plantation house has two stories with galleries at the front and rear and a large attic floor. The original kitchen has disappeared over the course of years.

This plantation house was one of the first on the island to be given a new purpose early on: in 1864 the Franciscan sisters from Roosendaal bought Habaai to establish a boarding school for upper-class Curaçaoan and South American girls. When a new building with the name Welgelegen was built for this purpose in 1867, Habaai became an orphanage. At the beginning of the twentieth century, courses in straw hat weaving were taught at the plantation house.

The hats were produced on a large scale, and by 1910 almost a fifth of the total island population was engaged in hat weaving.

After the orphanage closed in 1924, novices lived in the plantation house. The sisters ran a nursery on the site. The upper floor was rented to private individuals.

In 1965 the bishop received the plantation house on loan from the Franciscan sisters. It was restored and rebuilt into a retreat center. In the 1970s it was also a chic place for wedding parties, first Holy Communions and receptions. Rental income from these events maintained the plantation house until the diocese decided to keep the revenues for itself, leading to the house's gradual decline.

At the end of the last century, the nuns sold Habaai to the president of the local chapter of the Hells Angels. As a matter of fact, nothing was done to the plantation house for several years so the decline continued. The annexes which the nuns had built behind the manor in the nineteenth century collapsed, but fortunately the plantation house remained standing.

In 2005, Lusette and Herman Verboom bought Habaai. With guidance from the architect Maup Lanjouw, they restored the plantation house and initially inhabited the top floor. A year later they moved Gallery Alma Blou from Otrobanda to the plantation house. Habaai has since been a bustling center of culture popular with both the locals as well as tourists. There are continuous exhibitions of Curaçaoan and Caribbean art, and locally hand-crafted items are offered for sale. The atmospheric back terrace is ideal for intimate gatherings.

HATO

NOTICE.

THE subscriber would respectfully inform invalids, and others, who may visit Curaçao, that, owing to the want of such a place of refuge in this island, and to the sollicitations of visitors, he has been induced to open for their reception his residence, HATO. He has therefore resolved to spare neither pains nor expense to promote the comfort, health, and pleasure of his guests. His gardens and table will be furnished with whatever luxuries the West Indies afford.

TERMS.—Board and washing, together with use of horses, or horse and carriage $ 1. 50. per day.

M. RÖMER.

Plantation HATO,
Curaçao, 28th April 1843.

In recent decades, more and more plantation houses have been transformed into places where one can lodge or dine. Hato was among the early ones of such retreats because by the nineteenth century visitors could spend a few days there and enjoy the coolness of the garden with its running spring water.

Until 1696 Hato was a governmental livestock ranch where food for the slaves was also grown. It additionally served as a private home for the directors of the West India Company. In 1843 Michael Römer placed newspaper ads announcing that his estate, Hato, was available for a multi-day, luxurious stay. Ten years later, Frederik Pierre also praised the "crystalline creek" and the "beautiful mansion" in an advertisement. A night's sleep on the plantation included the use of the baths which would also be beneficial for good health. If desired, the guest could take all his meals at Hato.

In 1929 it was decided to build the current airport on the former Hato plantation. Later, Rudy Plaate, the singing greengrocer, grew vegetables on the plantation grounds for many years. He sold these vegetables first in his shop at Bloemhof and then at Zuikertuintje. In 2014 the property was leased to tenants who built a vineyard and and ran a bed and breakfast in the country house. This arrangement did not last long because in 2016 the airport terminated the contract.

HEL

Backer, Paradijs, Tevredenheid, Onverwacht

THE FIRST PLANTATION HOUSE WAS SET
ABLAZE BY THE ENGLISH IN 1805.

The plantation with the ominous name Hel (meaning Hell) was founded around 1718 by Adriaan Backer. Thomas François Paradis then bought the plantation in 1764, renamed it Tevredenheid (Contentment), and the name continued until the plantation was sold in 1832. Later, the Dutch version of the surname was applied and both the country house as well as the plantation were known as Paradijs (Paradise), usually with the footnote "popularly known as Hel".

The story goes that the estate was called Hel when it was inhabited by a couple who constantly argued with each other.

The first plantation house was set ablaze by the English in 1805, but in 1817 there was again a house, which served mainly as a country retreat. In the nineteenth century it was consistently offered as "country estate, a villa, or retreat".

In 1900 Hel became the property of Casper Perret Gentil who bought the plantation from the Römer family. His son Oscar became the owner in 1920, and he and his wife Miekie Rojer moved into the plantation house. After Oscar's death in 1946, Miekie continued to live there until her death in 1970. By that time the house had been sold to the island territory which used it for the Department of Sports (Sedreko). At the moment it is unoccupied.

HERMANUS
Oud Sint Marie

Since 2018 the old border post of the Hermanus and Meiberg plantations has been restored to its former glory along the road to Willibrordus. It was restored by Rensly Simon, and subsequently Herman Verboom and François van der Hoeven added the names in calligraphy.

Hermanus and Meiberg have almost always been in the hands of the same owner. One of the oldest owners was Hermanus Storck, hence the name Hermanus for this plantation house. Hermanus was, just like Jan Kok, a salt plantation, and until 1863 large numbers of slaves performed the heavy labor.

In the course of the slave revolt of 1795, one of its leaders, Louis Mercier, had the original house burnt down. The present two-storied house, with its hipped roof and continuous cornices typifies the architectural style of the second half of the nineteenth century. The section that connects perpendicularly to the house has a more traditional design with galleries. It is obvious that this part is older.

Because of their location near the sea, Shell wanted to buy both Hermanus and Meiberg in 1928 for the construction of a disposal facility. In the end, only Meiberg changed hands. The current owners use Hermanus as a weekend retreat. There are no longer cows, sheep or goats in the corral around the house, but there are geese and peacocks.

| 127

JAN KOK

Zevenhuizen

This plantation house bears the name of the founder of the plantation, Adriaan Kock. His name was altered first to Arrian and then to Jan. That is why Teenstra still refers to *Plantaadje Arrienkok* in the account of his travels of 1836.

This Adriaan was a master mason and one of the first settlers on the island. Around 1705 he built a house here that was initially named Zevenhuizen (Seven Houses), presumably because his was the seventh house in the area along with Oud Sint Marie (now Hermanus), Nieuw St. Marie (now Rif), Malpais, Sint Joris (later Siberie), San Sebastian, and Port Marie.

Adriaan planted beans for the garrison and, additionally, let cattle graze on the plantation. Later on Jan Kok became a well-known salt plantation, especially after 1832 when there was great demand for salt from Curaçao. The owner of Jan Kok created new saltpans, and in the 1840s the plantation counted eleven hectares where salt could be harvested. Nowadays flamingos from Bonaire feed in the former saltpans, and they have become a tourist attraction.

The house built by Adriaan Kock no longer exists. It must have already been a ruin in 1784, because the deed of sale in that year does not mention the well-known term: "with a building for housing". From construction traces one can deduce that a fire was the probable cause of the deterioration. Only the *mangasina* with its seventeenth-century façade remained. The cellar also survived the fire.

In 1784 the Venezuelan Silberio Cafiero purchased Jan Kok, along with the plantation Sint Joris, now known as Siberie. Cafiero took up residence in Siberie and therefore did not need a house at Jan Kok. Thus the burned-out house remained a ruin until in the middle of the nineteenth century Carel Zacharias de Haseth became its owner. He built the current plantation house on the remnants of the old house, placing it on a high terrace with galleries on both sides of the house.

In the twentieth century the plantation house took on a mainly recreational function. In 1948 veterinary surgeon Max Diemont purchased the ramshackle plantation house from the government and personally and thoroughly restored it with guidance from the architect Serge Alexeenko in the 1960s. It became a popular nightspot with a museum, a wine cellar and a dance floor next to the plantation house. In 1965, Diemont went on to buy the salt pans from the government since he believed that they formed an inseparable whole with the plantation house.

| 133

Under the ownership of Jeannette Leito, who owned the house from 1976 onward, its nightlife function more or less persisted. Leito gave tours of the property, provided meals, and parties could also be held at Jan Kok.

Since 1999, *stichting Monumentenzorg Curaçao* (Curaçao Heritage Foundation) has owned the entire Jan Kok plantation, including the plantation house and the salt pans. The now deceased Curaçaoan artist Nena Sanchez rented the plantation house from the Foundation. In it she housed her studio and a gallery with her colorful Caribbean paintings, thereby once again establishing Jan Kok as a tourist attraction.

36

JAN SOFAT

Jan Zoutvat, Vredenberg, Uylenburg

In 1715, the skipper Jan Houtvat bought the Uylenburg plantation as a dwelling where he could pass the days he spent on land. Its name was later distorted into Jan Sofat.

The tombstone of Hermanus Kikkert, the administrator of finance who died in 1854, was located in the family cemetery on the site and can now be found in the garden of the Curaçao Museum. Kikkert's son-in-law was the owner of Jan Sofat.

In 1862, the government bought Jan Sofat for district commissioner Ferguson. To that end the corn barn was converted into a barracks, the chicken coop was turned into a kitchen and the coach house with its toilet became a prison. As compensation Ferguson received a new lavatory, a luxury in those days.
Although the name Zoutvat would suggest otherwise, there were no salt pans. The plantation did provide fruit, vegetables and sorghum, but it was rather insignificant. According to Ferguson, the revenues did not compensate for the salaries of the farmers or the cost of transporting the crops to town. In the mid-twentieth century, the Sprockel heirs owned the property and leased the land for the construction of weekend houses at Spanish Water. Following the sale to Spanish Water Resort in 1969, the area was parceled out, leaving the plantation house hidden behind luxury villas.

JAN THIEL
Damasco

37

Arturo Perret Gentil - shon Tutu - can be regarded as the founder of the present-day tourist complex surrounding Jan Thiel bay. In 1915 he purchased the almost 400 hectare plantation including the plantation house from the heirs of David Vidal. In addition to expanding the eighteenth century salt pans, he also established the Vista Alegre seaside resort in 1924. The resort consisted of a wooden hotel, a bathhouse, and five vacation rentals. Visitors paid admission, and on the weekends Arturo provided musical entertainment.

Although the plantation was originally called Damasco, the salt pans in its vicinity and the plantation house were soon referred to by the name of its oldest known owner, Jan Thielen, whose ownership dates to the eighteenth century. The property retained its name even though the plantation was sold by Jan Thielen's heirs to Moses Penso in 1737. The saltpans seemed to have been a good investment, and they changed hands often owing to their profitability.

In the eighteenth century there were approximately forty slaves who were responsible for harvesting the cotton, growing the vegetables and fruit, and tending to the many goats, sheep, cows, and chickens. Not only was there salt but cotton, sorghum (*maishi chikí*), indigo, and several kinds of vegetables were also harvested. In 1816 the plantation's inventory counted "15 sacks of cotton seed". The plantation house would appear to have been built in the mid-eighteenth century since it is recorded in 1752 that construction supplies for a house were present on the plantation.

At the onset of the nineteenth century the plantation entered a period of decline. This deterioration came to an end when the Lauffer brothers bought Jan Thiel in 1834 and for forty-three years took good care of the estate, just as shon Tutu would from 1915 onward.

Shon Tutu was a hard worker and created a flourishing plantation thanks to the construction of dams. In 1929 the Perret Gentil family took up residence in the plantation house which had been outfitted with such modern conveniences as a bathroom.

In the 1970s Shon Tutu initiated the allotment of the plantation for the development of the Vista Royal project. Shortly thereafter he sold the remainder of the plantation, along with the plantation house, to the pension fund (APNA) which allowed him to spend the rest of his life there. Eventually, the APNA sold the plantation house plus a piece of land for a nominal sum to the Curaçao Heritage Foundation.

Lacking the funds for an urgent restoration, in 1997 the estate was leased for sixty years to the Dutch lawyer Leo Spigt on the condition that he restore the plantation house. That restoration occurred under the direction of architect Norbert Broos. Several structures were also restored, such as the cow barn, the cattle corrals and the site where the cows were milked. The milking buckets used to be stored inverted on sticks that fit into specifically designed holes.

The mansion eventually became a boutique hotel and retained this function when, in 2017, the current owners took over Jan Thiel. Having adopted the name Plantation Jan Thiel Lodge, they run the plantation house with the outbuildings as a bed and breakfast. So there is, just as in the past, life in and around the country house.

38 JANWÉ

Klein Zuurzak, Goed Begin

The name of the Janwé plantation house, which is surrounded by greenery and is also known as Jan Wee, is thought to be an abbreviation of the name of one of its eighteenth century residents: Jan or Jantje Wever. A subsequent owner was Carl Magnus Neuman, who, as a "captain of the Indians", had sat on the Bonaire government.

In 1839 he moved to Curaçao and bought the Goed Begin (Good Start) plantation. Thereafter, Janwé was probably used mainly as a country house. It was also a water plantation.

The next two owners, the shopkeeper John Henry Anthony Neuman and the "physician appointed for the colony" Corneille Hubert Jonckheer, owned more real estate on the island. For example, Jonckheer himself lived in the Breedestraat in Punda and may have used Janwé as a country house, or even as an investment: he bought the plantation in 1845 but sold it two years later to purchase the Bottelier plantation.

Neuman also owned more real estate, such as various houses on Pietermaai; later he became the owner of the Rust en Vrede (Peace and Quiet) plantation, known as well as De Vergenoeging (Contentment). Presumably he rented out Janwé.

In 1918 the Roman Catholic church bought the plantation intending to build a church with a parsonage and a school. Four years later, the first Holy Mass was dedicated in the plantation house. Mass continued to take place every Sunday until 1924 when the Sacred Heart Church of Janwé was completed and consecrated.

In the 1940s, the government bought back the plantation house and a small part of the land with the intention of starting up some farming. Despite objections that they were too close to the church cemetery, new wells were dug for water extraction. In 1954, Janwé was transferred from the Netherlands Antilles government to the Island Territory, which in turn transferred the plantation house to the Curaçao Heritage Foundation in 1960. The house was restored then and again in 2000. In the 1980s the plantation house served as the rectory of the church of Janwé. The Curaçao Heritage Foundation sold the plantation house in 2005.

Five years later, the current owner bought the plantation house and restored it within the next few years. He also added an extra space to the plantation house, accessible from the house through a modern glass corridor. The roof of this extension is black, while the plantation house has a red roof. In this way the owner wants to emphasize that it is a modern addition.

The rain reservoir next to the terrace is still intact, as is the coach house, which now serves as a hobby and laundry room. Some original doors can be found inside. An unusual feature is the new and floating mahogany staircase to the first floor.

JOONCHI

Joontje, Mon Repos, Quinta Edna

NEOCLASSICAL HOUSE WITH
CHARACTERISTIC SYMMETRY.

Joonchi is a typical example of a country retreat. In the course of the nineteenth century large country houses where one could escape hot weekends and summer months among leafy fruit trees were regularly built in existing "gardens". Because they were not plantation houses they had no *mangasinas* or other annexes.

In 1802 this land was owned by a certain Anna Cathalina Joontje so that is where the current name originated although later in the nineteenth century it was known as Mon Repos.

Benjamin Jesurun, in the last decade of the 1800s, bought the grounds in order to build this beautiful, neoclassical house with its characteristic symmetry. The house definitely does not resemble a Curaçaoan plantation house and would not look out of place on the Mediterranean. A beautiful entrance gate, in which a flowerpot with flowers is incorporated, affords access to the estate.

As a pastime Benjamin Jesurun planted trees near the plantation house and beautified the grounds and driveway. Just as at Groot Kwartier, which was owned by his brother Edward, he installed a large number of windmills.

| 147

Via an ingenious irrigation system, water was pumped up and led to a *baki* from which all the trees were irrigated. Every few months the baki was cleaned and algae removed. The children and their friends could then come and enjoy a swim in this improvised pool.

At the end of 1923 Henry Perret Gentil bought the plantation house, then called Quinta Edna, from Christiaan Winkel. He lived there with his wife Silvia and their children for a few years, but when the family moved to Switzerland for an extended period of time, the house was rented.

After Henry died his wife Silvia and three of their children lived there from the 1950s until her death in 1987; subsequently their son Casper Mario lived at Joonchi. In 1989 the heirs of Henry and Silvia sold the plantation house, and it was used as an office.

Following the last sale, the original square shape of the house disappeared. To create more office space, a substantial section in the same style was added at the rear. Behind the house and to its left, an almost identical new building with the same beautiful staircase, landing and balcony on the first floor was erected. Both houses, the old as well as the new, are well maintained.

The estate is still an oasis of calm in this busy residential area. Tall palms and other trees provide coolness and shade and a stream ripples to a pond. In this spot one can well imagine what some nineteenth-century retreats would have looked like.

KAS CHIKITU

Cas Chiquito, Gerustheid

The plantation Gerustheid has had a series of owners. For example, Mathias van der Dijs owned the plantation from 1800 to 1805 before buying Klein Malpais and later the much larger Savonet. Kas Chikitu, the small house, was probably built around 1850.

At the end of the nineteenth century when the plantation became the property of the Hypotheekbank (mortgage bank), the house gradually languished until the government bought Kas Chikitu in 1907 and turned it into a culture garden. An agriculturist moved into the refurbished plantation house, and experiments were done with various crops. After experimenting with aloe in the nineteenth century, rubber, banana, *laraha* trees and sisal were added. Palm trees, which provided the straw hat industry with its leaves, were also planted. The agricultural experiment ended in 1926 because the Colonial Council saw no benefit in it. In the second half of the last century, the house first served as a police station and an official residence. Subsequently, beginning in 1979, the island government accommodated the government doctors here. Former Prime Minister Whiteman, among others, had his practice there. When the government stopped providing general medical care in 2000, one of the GPs purchased the traditionally built plantation house with its two wide galleries. It still houses a general practice and is well maintained.

TUA RES AGITUR

DE STICHTING MONUMENTENZORG CURAÇAO
HEEFT DEZE PLAQUETTE AANGEBODEN ALS
BLIJK VAN WAARDERING VOOR INITIATIEF
EN BURGERZIN DIE DIT BOUWWERK VOOR
ONZE GEMEENSCHAP BEHIELDEN

KLEIN BLOEMHOF

Severeyn, Zefrin, Klein Bloempot

Klein Bloemhof can hardly be called a plantation. The estate was used as an investment or as a country retreat and not for growing produce or raising cattle. At most, a few fruits or vegetables were destined for town. In 1834, except for one donkey, cattle were no longer present. According to Wim Renkema, resident of Klein Bloemhof in the 1970s and author of "The Curaçao Plantation in the Nineteenth Century", Klein Bloemhof did not play a major role in the agricultural history of the island.

The name Severeyn refers to the owners between 1816 and 1925: Abraham Severijn, his children Ebbetje and Johannes, and their heirs. Zefrin refers to John's wife Cathalina Zefrien.

The small original house was built in the neoclassical style fashionable on the island in the second half of the nineteenth century. Typical is the symmetrical façade with a pediment on columns, giving the house the allure of a plantation house. The house is a *kas di kaha* and has two buildings abutting one another, each with a hipped roof. The decoration in the pediment consists of a vase with flowers. In the 1980s a bedroom with an en suite bath and a covered porch were added on to the rear of the house. In 1997 the house received a new owner, and it is well maintained.

KLEIN KWARTIER

Vrede

Since 2012 the Curaçao Lions Club has rented this small manor house for its meetings. The house is also rented out for parties and events which the large garden and rear terrace lend themselves to perfectly.

Around 1900 Klein Kwartier, owned by the Senior family, was an important *laraha* plantation with approximately one thousand orange trees. The peels of the fruit were processed into the well-known Curaçao liqueur which pharmacists Edgar Senior and Isaac Chumaceiro distilled behind their Botika Excelsior on the Heerenstraat (see Chobolobo).

In 1927 the government bought the plantation to house the National Water Supply Service. The company's director, Richard "Hensey" Beaujon, occupied the manor house with his family. In the 1920s and 1930s his son Jan Jacob "Japa" Beaujon, who would later be lieutenant governor of the Windward Islands, and the writer Boelie van Leeuwen, son of the district master, played among the laraha trees. During the rainy season they also swam in the dams.

In later years government doctors were stationed in the manor house. In 1965, the island gifted the manor house to the Curaçao Heritage Foundation which rented it out to Donny Bakhuis. Subsequently, the manor house underwent a major restoration in which the original roof and the three dormer windows disappeared. Thus, the house lost part of its historic character.

KLEIN SANTA MARTHA

DURING THE MAJOR SLAVE REVOLT OF 1795
THE PLANTATION WAS THE SCENE OF AN
UNSETTLING OCCURRENCE.

**In 1698 Aron Levi Maduro, one of the first
Sephardic Jews to come to Curaçao, owned
this plantation. In those years sugar cane
was cultivated and divi divi trees grew on the
property.**

Klein Santa Martha was a prosperous plantation.
When Matthias Schotborg owned it in 1819, the
plantation had 99 slaves. Some tended to the
sheep, cows, donkeys, and chickens while others
worked as apprentice cooks or salesgirls in town.
Throughout all this time Klein Santa Martha
remained an important salt plantation alongside
the other plantations that got their salt from
the saltpans in Santa Martha bay: Groot Santa
Martha and San Nicolas. During the major slave
revolt of 1795 the plantation was the scene of
an unsettling occurrence: the resident tutor
Sabel was the only white inhabitant of Klein
Santa Martha at that moment. The rebellious
slaves, led by Pedro Wacao, tied him to a horse
and dragged him to Fontein where he was
subsequently murdered.

Much later, in 1937, the government assumed
ownership of the plantation in order to promote
agriculture and cattle breeding following plans

designed by former governor Oscar Helfrich. The plantation house came to be inhabited by the Dutch farmer Wietse de Vries. Helfrichdorp was the name given to the village specifically built to foster this project where farmers could live and learn the trade.

In the end the project failed, and in 1954 the plantation was put on the market. It didn't sell and was thus used for years as a holiday camp, and in 1965 a family lived there. When they left and squatters moved in, the plantation house started to visibly deteriorate. It was only a skeleton when the government donated it to *Monumentenzorg Curaçao* (Curaçao Heritage Foundation) in 1995.

The restoration was initiated in 2012, and two years later the premises opened as a boutique hotel. Architects Anko van der Woude and Cas Aalbers drew up a restoration plan that did justice to the historic, presumably eighteenth-century building by respecting its central core and both front and back galleries. The nineteenth-century additions of white cornerstones were also maintained.

The restoration took into account the requirements of the modern-day tourist, and evidence of this is visible mostly in the house's interior. In the house proper there are four hotel rooms with private bathrooms while the fifth hotel room is housed in the former stable. The reception area, the lounge and a library occupy the erstwhile *sala* and the two galleries. The free-standing kitchen with its built-in fireplace has been properly restored. What used to be the *mangasina* has been redesigned into a luxury apartment.

Not only can you sleep in this modern-looking building, you can also dine on its terrace. Due to its elevation, the plantation house offers a splendid view of Santa Martha bay. This must be the same view enjoyed by Aron Levi Maduro in his day.

KLEIN ST. JORIS

Chinchó Chikí

In 1879 this plantation was the last to join the merger of the plantations Oostpunt, Fuik, Duivelsklip and Oranjeberg. Since then, these plantations have been in the hands of the same family. Together they cover ten percent of Curaçao's land area. The five plantations are popularly called Oostpunt.

In 1635, the first Dutch farmer, Laurens Pietersz, and his two servants cultivated the land here. After unsuccessfully sowing rye, wheat and tobacco, Pietersz soon opted for a permanent position at the West India Company.

After Pietersz, arable farming and animal husbandry were carried out at Klein Sint Joris, and initially even sugar cane was cultivated. In 1910 the plantation had a "forest of heavy and solemnly waving coconut palms". Even today goats and sheep are kept at Klein Sint Joris and vegetables are grown. This makes it the only operational plantation remaining.

The plantation house was probably built before 1662, although it must be noted that the kitchen area is the oldest. The cistern and the *mangasina* were added last, in 1884. It is striking that the tower is not directly adjacent to the terrace, as is the case with the other country houses with one or more towers. Here the tower served as a coach house in which the *kitoki* (carriage) was parked. The coachman had his living quarters upstairs.

The plantation house is inhabited and was restored in 1981. Since then it has been well maintained. The entire site, encompassing the Klein Sint Joris, Oranjeberg, Fuik, Duivelsklip and Oostpunt plantations, is privately owned and absolutely not accessible to the public.

KLEIN SINT MICHIEL

Sami Chiki

Klein Sint Michiel is an old plantation that borders the *saliña* of Sint Michiel. From the outset, the harvesting of salt in that saliña was an important activity at the plantation. The first owner of the plantation was Moses Levi Maduro who arrived on the island in 1672.

The merchant and ship chandler Genereux J.R. de Lima bought the plantation with its house, inventory and slaves in 1853. He was the son of a former slave girl, Regina Jesurun, who lived openly with the Jewish merchant Isaac Abinun de Lima. She had a shop in the Keukenstraat and also owned several houses. Although Genereux was only lightly colored, it is still noteworthy that in 1867, despite being illegitimate and Roman Catholic, he attained membership of the Colonial Council. Additionally, he held various other senior positions. The date 1862, engraved into the façade of the country house, refers to the year De Lima reconstructed and restored the house.

The now almost square plantation house has a beautiful double staircase with an openwork balustrade leading to the landing. The gable stone with an image of the archangel Michael above the side terrace door is not original but was brought from France by the family in the 1960s. There are still several old buildings on the site such as a *mangasina* with yellow brick flooring, a supervisor's cottage, corrals, and a water reservoir.

In 1884, De Lima's widow sold the plantation to Pieter Gorsira. Klein Sint Michiel remained in the hands of this family for over a hundred years. Michael and Marieta Brown Gorsira, Pieter's grandchildren, decorated the house with beautiful antique furniture and paintings, some of which came from the museum that their uncle Cornelis Gorsira furnished on Ararat. According to Ozinga, they still ran the plantation like a traditional cattle farm in the 1950s.

Following the sale of the cows in the 1960s, they continued to keep sheep and goats and farmed for a long time afterward. The plantation also had a garden with mainly mango and sapodilla trees and various freshwater wells. The large indigo container to the side of the salt pans confirms that the blue dye was once produced at Klein Sint Michiel.

After being purchased by Mr and Mrs De Haas in 2002, the plantation house and its annexes were gradually restored to their original condition, as much as possible. Twelve years later, the architect Cees den Heijer and his family moved into the plantation house. His modern adjustments to the interior were made in such a way that the twenty-first century additions to the original building are clearly visible. The kitchen floor, for instance, still consists of yellow bricks that probably originate from the eighteenth-century house.

He followed the same principle on the site of the plantation: Den Heyer built ultramodern villas for sale or rent that contrast sharply with the old plantation house thereby clearly showing that this is a contemporary addition to an old Curaçao plantation.

KNIP

Kenepa

It stands to reason that the Tula Museum, with its focus on the history of slavery, is located in this beautiful old plantation house. It was here that in 1795 the great slave uprising, led by the slave Tula, began. On view on the first floor is a long list of punishments, such as lashings or imprisonment lasting for days, that slaves could expect for certain offenses.

According to the date in the top façade, the house was either built or rebuilt in 1830. The plantation, surrounded by fairly high hills, is much older; in 1693 it had already been sold with grazing rights for an indefinite amount of cattle. In subsequent centuries, Knip remained an important cattle plantation. In the mid-twentieth century its now empty corrals were filled with hundreds of goats.

In 2018, with support from the Prins Bernhard Culture Fund Caribbean Region, the Archeology Study Group consolidated a number of old border posts. These barriers are situated between Lagun and Knip, as well as two border posts on the Westpunt side which were most likely part of an entrance gate.

The same study group discovered indigo containers on the plantation grounds in 2014. Indigo, for the extraction of blue dye, was cultivated well into the eighteenth century in Curaçao. There is still an old *pos di pia*, a walk-in well, on the property.

When Jannetje van der Meulen, the owner of Knip, died in 1832, the inventory showed that the house was lavishly decorated with mahogany furniture, paintings, trinkets, and mirrors. By Curaçao standards the plantation also had an enormous number of slaves totaling 128 Negroes and one Mulatto.

For a long time after van der Meulen's death the plantation house was only intermittently inhabited, but when the Muskus family took possession of the plantation house in the twentieth century it came to life again. Although Richard Muskus, its owner from 1938 onward, did not live in the plantation house, he did spend long weekends there with his family and guests. At that time, just like a century earlier, the house was furnished with original antiques. Muskus had the plantation house restored in 1939, as can be seen on the façade.

Richard was not the first Muskus to own Knip. His father, Ridchard Frederik, had also owned the house. In 1922 he invited snail expert Horace Burrington Baker to Knip and the latter decided to name one of the snails after Ridchard Muskus: the *Tudora muskusi*. A subspecies of the *Cerion uva* snail was given the name *knipensis*.

In the 1930s and for decades thereafter, the boy scouts regularly camped at Knip, and one can still see the ruins of their old clubhouse. In Richard's day Kleine Knipbaai was a private beach where guests of the family were allowed. Other guests were also welcomed. As the agent for a number of large shipping companies, Richard often brought ship captains to Knip.

In 1975, Muskus sold the plantation to the Island Territory which promised to transfer it, along with the plantation house, to the Curaçao Heritage Foundation in 1983. Following a costly restoration in 1985, the Curaçao Heritage Foundation had to wait until 1995 before it received the leasehold of Knip and could rent it out.

KONINGSPLEIN

47

This plantation was especially important for its abundance of water. Between 1875 and 1877 Isaac Pinedo offered well water that "the public has been drinking here for a series of years and that he delivered to the garrison throughout 1873 and 1874 without any complaint". As evidenced by birth announcements, Pinedo and his wife Rebecca lived at Koningsplein from 1859 until 1862.

In 1884 Koningsplein was put up for sale "koe oen paleis di un kas" (with a palace of a house) along with two large reservoirs and wells that supplied water all year round. The new owner, Pieter Hendrik Maal, allowed his small livestock to roam around Schapeneiland (Sheeps' Island) which was part of the plantation. Well into the early twentieth century, wooden ferries brought water from the reservoirs to Scharloo. Maal's son Jozef "Jojo" Maal used the plantation house for weekends and parties.

In 1923 Jojo Maal sold Koningsplein to Shell which was interested in the Schapeneiland in the Schottegat. It was connected to the mainland, and in 1941 Shell built the dry dock there.

The plantation house was inhabited until the 1970s by Hendrik Smeins and Isedora Aurora Craane and their 24 children. They were probably the last inhabitants of that area. In 1984 Koningsplein became the headquarters of Curinde (Curaçao Industrial & International Trade Development), the heart of Curaçao's Free Zone.

| 173

48

KORAAL TABAK

Koraal Tabak was one of the large plantations owned by the Dutch West India Company (WIC) around 1700. As the name implies, tobacco was also grown. In 1636, the WIC director reported to the Messrs. XIX that the "tobacco seed in our garden at Chinchorro" yielded little. He might have been referring to Sint Joris, which lies east of Koraal Tabak.

The nineteenth-century plantation house consists of two units with a spacious room at the front. At the rear a kitchen, among other things, has been added. The house stands on a little hill which provides it with a nice view. Unfortunately, two large *mangasinas* and cattle corrals that were once situated next to the plantation house have been razed.

Mid-twentieth century the Bakhuis family came into possession of the plantation. In 1963 Hugo Bakhuis opened *Wonderful Beach* at Sint Jorisbaai; there was also a recreation area with weekend homes, bridle paths, a football field, and a volleyball court. There was a restaurant in the plantation house and Bakhuis, also known as *Mr. Wonderful*, even initiated a special bus line from Punda.

The venture was not a success: the recreation center closed two years later. There remained a drag race track on the plains of the north coast that was exploited for years. Until this century diabase was extracted at the former plantation, and the site was also used as a garbage dump.

Koraal Tabak has recently been sold to investors who intend to restore the plantation house.

MORGENSTER

'A WELL-APPOINTED HOUSE AND ANNEXES'.

From the outset this little plantation house has been offered for sale as a garden or country retreat. In 1859, for example, when it had "a well-appointed house and annexes". Included in the purchase were two draft horses, a wagon and three carts. In the following years the house was regularly available for rent.

According to Father Brenneker, there was a cemetery situated on a little hill behind the plantation house where people from the neighborhood were buried, but by 1972 it had disappeared.

The political party MAN bought the plantation house in the early 1980s from the Beaujon family. According to the first party leader Don Martina, Morgenster was on the verge of collapsing. The house was restored and officially put to use as the party's *sede* in 1983. When two years later this MAN headquarters was destroyed by a fire, the heavily damaged left side of the house was rebuilt.

The house could do with a fresh coat of paint since MAN established a new party headquarters on the Rooseveltweg in 2016.

MOUNT PLEASANT

Malpais, Groot Malpais

In 1810, twelve years after purchasing the plantation, its owner, Gerard Duyckink, legally decreed that his plantation would henceforth be called Mount Pleasant. This is understandable considering that the original name Malpais (bad land) does not sound very promising for a plantation. Currently, the plantation house is once again known as Malpais.

Salt harvesting and animal husbandry were especially important for Malpais. That changed at the beginning of the last century when 200 hectares of sisal were cultivated. In 1918, the First Sisal Culture Society planted a quarter of the fields of Malpais with sisal and purchased a defibring machine. At the time, the Sisal Society was led by Gijsbert d'Aumale, Baron van Hardenbroek who lived in the Papaya plantation house. Despite the enthusiasm for sisal cultivation, the company went bankrupt in 1922, and in 1924 Shell bought the plantation. With Shell's permission, the *Birgen di Rosario* Foundation wanted to establish a retirement home at Malpais in 1943. Due to the high renovation costs, however, Santa Catharina was rented instead, followed by a move to Huize Welgelegen less than a year later. In the 1960s Dutch farmers managed the plantation house. The Keijzer milk company advertised the sale of fresh milk, butter, cheese and yogurt from Malpais. The plantation house is now owned by a Christian church and was, for some time, a children's home. There is also a church building on the grounds. Two years ago this exceptional eighteenth-century plantation house, with its baroque side façades and five baroque dormer windows at the front, was designated a protected monument. The owners intend to restore it.

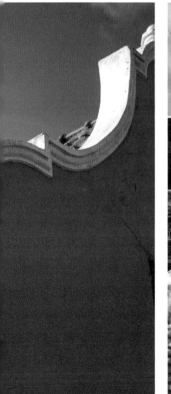

51

OOST JONGBLOED

Boventuin, Vergenoeging

The oldest known owner, skipper Jan Jongbloet, called the plantation Boventuin (Upper Garden), but everyone else called it Jongbloed. The original Jongbloed manor house was already derelict in the early nineteenth century.

The current manor house was built a century later by Cornelis Colonis Sprockel. His son Wiles Oliver later added a cross wing. The house is now called Oost Jongbloed to avoid confusion with the old Jongbloed manor house.

In 1858 Cornelis Sprock and his eponymous son bought the Jongbloed plantation. Five years later, the elder Cornelis Sprock was the sole owner. He was married, but soon after his arrival on the island in 1844 he had begun living with the slave Josephina Victorina Sprothouars, also known as Francinette, whom he bought in 1847. Together they had seven children who were given the family names of Sprothouars, Sprockel or Sprock after their release from slavery.

In 1873, Sprock sold Jongbloed to Francinette on the condition that he could continue to run the plantation. After her death, one of their children, the above-mentioned Cornelis Colonis Sprockel, became the new owner of Jongbloed and Jongbloed still belongs to Sprock's descendants. Cornelis' granddaughter has lived in the manor house, which she had restored in 2010, since 1965.

PANNEKOEK
Kleine Kloof

This plantation is named for its probable founder, Gerrit Pannekoek. Due to a lack of fresh water, the plantation was insignificant. For that reason, in 1790 there stood only an old, dilapidated, straw hutch. Given the difference in purchase price between 1804 and 1830, the current manor house must have been built in those years.

From 1863 to 1871, district commissioner Van Dam lived on Pannekoek. Willem da Costa Gomez subsequently bought the manor house. He first lived there himself and then rented it out from 1880 onward (see Dokterstuin). In 1914 the government bought the manor house to accommodate the government doctor of the fourth and fifth districts. Water damage in the aftermath of Hurricane Hazel in 1954 made Pannekoek uninhabitable. Upon its restoration, the White Yellow Cross used it as a children's vacation camp from 1960 until 1962. After that Pannekoek became a camping center where the Youth Center Curaçao organized conferences for young leaders and other events.

Prior to its renewed use, it was restored by architect Henk Nolte who made every effort to preserve the original character of the manor house such as keeping the old oven in the kitchen. In 1976, the Youth Center assumed management of the manor house. A subsequent restoration and expansion, again by Nolte, took place in 1982. The manor house is still a camping center.

PAPAYA
Weltevrede

In 1810 Gerard Duyckinck separated a piece of land from the Malpais plantation and sold it, under the name Weltevrede, to Christoph Hoyer. The name Papaya came later.

In 1862 the small plantation, including cattle and two slaves, became the property of the former slave John Paul Rib. Freed at the age of thirty-three in 1842, Rib had his own carpentry business. It is not known if the plantation house already existed or if Rib built it. The house has three hipped roofs, connected one behind the other, typical of the second half of the nineteenth century.

In 1897 Julius Helmijr bought Papaya. With his family of eleven children he lived in the plantation house and built extra bedrooms behind the house for the boys. Later, in the mid-1930s, his children and grandchildren used Papaya as a country retreat. They took turns spending weekends there. There was no electricity; water was supplied by the reservoir and the well. During the summer holidays it was often packed with family. One of the Helmijr sons also lived at Papaya for a year.

Following Julius Helmijr's death in 1942, landowner Johannes Hendrick Jonckheer bought the plantation house in 1944.

At Papaya in the 1980s, a Dutch farming family raised pigs meant for slaughter. After their return to the Netherlands, the plantation house remained unoccupied for several years until it became a restaurant in 1993. In this century it served as a shelter for addicts until 2017.

PARERA

Berg Carmel

The Parera plantation house has housed the Public Works Department for almost a century. In 1928, Henry and Oscar Perret Gentil sold the house and the surrounding land to the government. The brothers had taken over the plantation house in 1908 from their father, who, in turn, had purchased the house three years earlier.

Oscar Perret Gentil and his wife Miekie lived briefly in the manor house before moving to Hel in 1920.

The name Parera comes from the oldest known owner, the widow Parera or Pereira, who sold the plantation in 1745. The house was built on the plantation's highest point in the early nineteenth century.

The grounds of the plantation lay at the Schottegat, where its few salt pans yielded little. Furthermore, Parera did not contribute much as a plantation. In 1844 it had to be auctioned off, and the wealthy Jacob Abraham Jesurun became its new owner.

From then on the manor houses surrounding the Schottegat were mainly used as country retreats. Presumably Jesurun "modernized" the appearance of his country house at that time by adding classical dentils and beautiful drapery decorations to the cornices of the galleries.

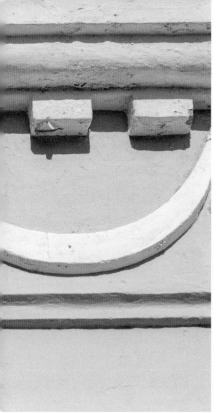

POS CABAI
Zuikerthuin

Pos Cabai was a small plantation of only eight hectares, a few slaves and a limited amount of cattle.

Once it had a large well, but in 1830 the owner of Pos Cabai was allowed to seal it up because the water was no longer drinkable. The name Pos Cabai (horse well) refers to the equestrian corps, founded in 1635, that was stationed in the area.

A house was first mentioned in the 1821 deed of purchase, but, as often happened, additions were made to the house at a later date. Just as at Brakkeput Meimei and Bona Vista, what was originally the front of the house has become its rear.

Visitors to the Pain Clinic and Cosmetic Center Curaçao, presently located in the plantation house, enter the building through a spacious front terrace flanked by left and right wings added in the late nineteenth century. The motif of the cornice with its beautiful drapery decorations extending even onto the chimney also dates from the nineteenth century. The cistern is partially located under the terrace.

In the 1950s, Pos Cabai, like its neighbor Bever, belonged to Benny Maduro. Later it was occupied by several offices.

RONDE KLIP

RONDE KLIP WAS OFFERED FOR SALE WITH "A RES-
PECTABLE INVENTORY, KNOWN AS ONE OF THE BEST
CATTLE RANCHES ON CURAÇAO".

**This classicist plantation house is often called the most beautiful
of Curaçao. The name, which means "Round Cliff", comes from the
mountain in the middle of the plantation. This mountain is round
and has a limestone plateau. The populace refers to it as *Ronduklé*.**

The monumental neoclassical building with its strikingly large
pediment on columns along the top floor was probably built
against a slope circa 1850. That would have happened when Doctor
Waters Forbes was the owner. Forbes was married to Sara Elisabeth
Berch who died in the plantation house in 1857. Supervision of the
plantation was left to their son Jacob. In 1872 and 1875, Ronde Klip
was offered for sale with "a respectable inventory, known as one
of the best cattle ranches on Curaçao", along with the plot of land,
Poppo. Jacob Jeosuah Naar bought the plantation in May of 1876.
This was the same Naar who built the Naar Theater at Pietermaai in
1871.

Just as at the Tafelberg, phosphate was discovered here in 1886,
but the quantity and quality could not compare to the phosphate
mined at Tafelberg. In 1943 the government bought the plantation
and the plantation house. First there was talk of the establishment
of a hotel or bungalow park. Later, there was some discussion about
establishing an educational institution for girls led by the sisters
of Bethany. In the early 1950s the Federation of Antillean Youth
Services adopted this plan, but it was never implemented.

In the meantime, the Island government assumed ownership of the plantation house in 1954 and, according to the newspaper *Amigoe*, the plantation house was still in good shape and seemed well maintained. The house was loaned to The Antillean Boy Scout Association for use as its headquarters and training center. From the 1950s to the 1970s Youth Services organized holiday camps in and around Ronde Klip.

In 1978 the house still looked good. That year it served as the backdrop for the American film *Firepower* starring Sophia Loren, O.J. Simpson, and James Coburn. Ten years later, there were plans for prisoners to renovate the plantation house into a shelter for the homeless and drug addicts. These plans never materialized, and advocates for these monuments grew increasingly irritated at the gradual decline of the plantation house. In 1993 Jacky Voges, chairman of the Curaçao Heritage Foundation, stated that 'plantation house Ronde Klip is gracefully collapsing'. A year later, the plantation house was given to the Curaçao Heritage Foundation.

| 195

In 2002, under the supervision of the architect Anko van der Woude, the plantation house was restored and made suitable for habitation. To maintain historical integrity, a load-bearing structure of wood and tiles replaced the concrete floor, just as it was in the past. Although the plantation house looks impressive from the outside, it is only 4.5 meters deep, so there was not enough room for all of the bedrooms. During the restoration bedrooms on concrete pillars were added onto the back of the plantation house and connected to the historic structure via a short landing. The colors of the new building correspond with those of the plantation house, as does the shape of its roof. It is obvious that this is a modern, twenty-first-century addition.

ROOI CATOOTJE

Rust en Vrede

Rooi Catootje beautifully unifies the nineteenth and twenty-first centuries. The nineteenth century plantation house is appointed with antique furniture and radiates the past. In 2010 the last owner of the estate, Ena Dankmeijer-Maduro (1920-2016), had an ultra-modern, mostly glass library built right next to the original house. It holds her father's collection of Judaica and Antilliana. Together the two buildings form the unity envisioned by the then nonagenarian.

The Rooi Catootje plantation, which takes its name from a dry riverbed (rooi) that runs along the eastern border of the property, was established in the middle of the eighteenth century. Along with chickens and other poultry goats and sheep grazed in the public pastures, and in the garden coconut, papaya, mango, tamarind, and lemon trees grew.

As a result of some very dry years in the early nineteenth century the number of livestock decreased and the plantation diminished in importance until Rooi Catootje gradually became a weekend retreat for well-to-do merchants. It is presumably around that time, circa 1820, that the core of the current plantation house was constructed. When Salomon (S.E.L) Maduro took ownership of the house in 1853, he enlarged it by adding a second story to the core.

In 1933 Ena Dankmeijer's father, Salomon A.L. Maduro, became the new owner. He lived in Scharloo with his wife and daughter, but traditionally Rooi Catootje provided relief on warm weekends and during the summer months. In 1952 his daughter Ena and her husband, Emile Dankmeijer, moved into the house.

Beginning in his youth, Ena's father Salomon, nicknamed Mongui, had collected anything he could find related to the Antillean islands and/or Judaism: books, newspaper clippings, postage stamps, periodicals, invitations, menus, theater playbills, etc. After his death in 1967, his widow and daughter began entertaining the idea of housing his collections in a library. In 1969 Ena and her husband Emile moved into an architecturally ultra-modern house on the leafy grounds of the plantation. This house is now a children's museum. The plantation house was then empty and presented the ideal location for the S.A.L. (Mongui) Maduro Library.

The collection kept increasing because Ena tirelessly acquired newly published books. The plantation house eventually grew too small and the search for a larger building was initiated. It was astonishing that the elderly Ena opted for a hypermodern building that was to rise up next to the plantation house without dominating it. The architects Lyongo Juliana and Cees den Heyer made use of the natural slope and built the library partly underground so that the volume of the building does not stand out. It is a contemporary addition to a historic Curaçaoan monument. And what is most special is that from the new building one can still see the harbor just like Mongui Maduro saw it from the terrace of the plantation house.

History thus remains intact. To this day, for example, one can find in the *sala* of the plantation house the table where in 1954 Dutch, Surinamese and Antillean politicians held the preparatory talks for the Round Table Conference, which led to the Statute of the Kingdom of the Netherlands.

58 | RUST EN VREDE

De Vergenoeging

Since the last century Rust en Vrede (Peace and Quiet) has been the property of the Island Territory which used it as the official residence for the district master until the early 1960s. In the 1930s, for example, Piet van Leeuwen, the father of the writer Boelie van Leeuwen, lived in this plantation house that dates to the second half of the nineteenth century. His successor was Herman Schotborgh.

Later, the Island Territory housed the government doctors in Rust and Vrede; first Dr Gorsira and later Dr Rauchbaar who lived there with his family until 1990. He had his private practice at home and the government practice diagonally across from the church of Santa Rosa. In front and behind Rust en Vrede there were deep gardens that Dr Rauchbaar fenced off with cactus hedges. The back garden was accessible via two staircases which are hardly recognizable these days.

After Rauchbaar's departure, there was a lot of interest in the plantation house, but the government did nothing with it except for bricking up the windows and doors. As a result, Rust en Vrede is only a shadow of the former plantation house, and its decline continues mercilessly. In 2002 it officially became a protected monument.

SALIÑA ABOU
Genoegen Is Het Al

Since 1726 this plantation has changed hands 28 times. The name also changed regularly. After being called Goed Heenkomen, Ongegund, De Soutpan, and Genoegen Is Het Al, a 1837 "for sale" notice states the current name as Saliña Abou.

The plantation house likely dates from the end of the eighteenth century when the mulatto Juana Maria Levy owned it; she herself lived in the Hel plantation house. At the sale following her death in 1803, there was mention of a plantation house with eight chairs, a large table, a sideboard with a small ewer, and a pantry.

Willem Bakhuis bought the plantation in 1923. At that time, the front terrace was still made of yellow bricks over which cement tiles would later be placed. In addition, the country house had creaking wooden floors throughout.

In the mid-twentieth century, most of the grounds of the former plantation were sold for the construction of the Dr. Albert Schweitzer School and the St. Paulus College. The rest was parceled out so that the country house is now crammed between houses and offices. Mid 2007 the architects Anko van der Woude and Cees den Heijer renovated the plantation house and added a modern pergola to its rear. Today, Saliña Abou houses a daycare center.

A small part of the Saliña Abou plantation was already sold in 1895. This plot, along with a residence, a coach house, a *mangasina*, and a well was given the name Saliña. The Saliña plantation house was demolished in 2013.

SALIÑA ARIBA

Stadsrust

A sale advertisement from 1877 called the courtyard of this plantation a pleasure garden "especially conveniently located for someone who has to live in such a place as well as for the wealthy man who desires a Paradise close to the city". The sale included a house, three annexes, two wells and a cistern.

The buyer was the unfortunate Johannes Rojer who owned various plantations, none of which were profitable. He only owned Saliña Ariba for a mere few months before he found himself forced to live in a straw hut and plow his own land.

Primarily a country retreat in the nineteenth century, the plantation house was occupied by the Leon family in the twentieth century. In the 1930s and 1940s various people worked at planting food for the cows, horses, and goats. Using dams, rainwater was collected for this purpose. There were sapodillas and coconut palms in the courtyard. Any excess was sold in town.

The last occupant, a grandson of Shon Benny Leon, sold the house in 2017 to a project developer for the purpose of building an over fifty residential community on the grounds surrounding the plantation house. The plantation house will serve as a common area. Thus the site will once again, just as a century ago, be suitable for the "wealthy man who wants a Paradise close to the city".

SAN JUAN

Sint Jan

THE NAME SAN JUAN ALREADY EXISTED AMONG THE SPANIARDS, AND THE PLANTATION IS AMONG THE OLDEST OF THE ISLAND.

The San Juan plantation house exudes the atmosphere of yesteryear. Not only is the exterior reminiscent of its appearance a century ago, but, due to its decoration with antique furniture and the yellow bricks on the floor of the *sala*, a visitor feels transported to the past. That is why a number of scenes in the 2012 film *Tula The Revolt* about the 1795 slave rebellion were filmed here. In the film the plantation house was used as captain Westerholt's headquarters.

The name San Juan already existed among the Spaniards, and the plantation is among the oldest of the island. It was founded by Matthias Beck, vice-director of the Dutch West India Company prior to 1662. In the same century there were fields of millet, indigo, cotton and sugar cane. Furthermore, the plantation had a large number of livestock. The salt pans produced almost nothing, but as evidenced by an advertisement in 1850, it seems that lime, "slaked with fresh water", was sold. At the time of the sale to the future Dutch West India Company director Albert Kikkert in 1792, a forge and a carpenter's shop, both with their appurtenances, were included in the purchase;

also included were a sugar mill and several additional windmills, shoemaker's tools, and the contents of the plantation house. A distillery formed part of the plantation as well. No doubt rum was made there from the harvested sugar cane which was surely cultivated until the beginning of the nineteenth century. There were then thirteen slaves whereas in 1828 there were no fewer than 124 slaves at work on the plantation.

In 1800, due to the arrival of the English, the plantation's owner, Kikkert, left for Europe to support the Batavian Republic's fight against England. His wife, Anna Maria van Uytrecht, and their children stayed in Curaçao, but the yields from the plantations (the family also owned Pannekoek) were disappointing due to insufficient rain and looting by the English troops.

Kikkert's wife sold San Juan, and in 1806 Matthias Schotborgh became its new owner. Through his brother, Jacob van der Linde Schotborgh, San Juan has remained in the hands of the Schotborgh family to this day. Parcels of land have occasionally been sold. Dr P.H. "Gungu" Maal, for example, purchased a parcel in 1941 and proceeded to farm there after building dams regulating the water flow.

A special feature of the plantation house is the aqueduct that rests on a row of arches and leads the water from the house to the rain reservoir. The entrance stairs are made up of small yellow bricks and the house has an eighteenth-century hipped roof: a hipped roof that turns into a single-sloped pent roof above the four galleries. Furthermore, there are still Dutch sash windows between the gallery and the core of the house.

In 2015, the Archeological Study Group found the remains of an old border gate. Engraved in the yellow bricks of the two gate posts are the words "Gr St Jan" and "Oost Trankeer". The gate marked the border between the San Juan and Cas Abou plantations.

62 | SAN NICOLAS

This plantation house looks just the way it has since its construction in the eighteenth century: isolated, elevated, and affording a panoramic view of Santa Martha Bay. There were fields of indigo, slaves gathered divi divi pods and cut down dyewood, and cattle grazed. But of utmost importance was the salt harvest from the bay of Santa Martha. After some research the discovery of coal in the early twentieth century proved disappointing.

The plantation house features a water tank with saddle roof that is partly sunk in the terrace. Adjacent to it is a bathhouse where people could bathe with rainwater. Of particular note is the post on the terrace which held the slave bell heralding the start and end of the working day.

In the mid-twentieth century, San Nicolas belonged to shon Cai Winkel who spent holidays and occasionally weekends there with his entire family and many guests. They slept on cots. In the daytime people walked to one of the many beaches, and in the evening they played games. Livestock farming was still practiced, and on special occasions *kabritu* was served.

John Broek bought the plantation in 1980. He had plans for a tourist resort with holiday villas, tennis courts, swimming pools, a childrens' playground and an exclusive restaurant called Port San Nicolas. These ambitious plans have since changed, but the plantation house has been restored.

SAN SEBASTIAN

From 1845 until well into the twentieth century, this plantation house, which features the year 1754 on its façade, was almost uninterruptedly in the possession of the Statius Muller family. In 1849 August Leberegt Statius Muller, however, lived at Siberie, which was also his property.

Thus San Sebastian was empty, when Father Ledel from Buitenbosch, later Willibrordus, was homeless: his parsonage and church had yet to be built. Statius Muller, therefore, let him live at San Sebastian until 1853. Ledel said Mass in a straw hut.

| 215

Starting in 1863 August's son Hendrik, district commissioner, lived at San Sebastian, then owned by the government. According to Hendrik, the roof was in dire need of repairs at the end of 1868 because even a little bit of rainfall soaked the food in the pantry. In 1869 the government again put the plantation house on the market.

August Leberegt planted nopal cacti at both Siberie and San Sebastian. At the end of the century, his daughters, then owners of the plantation house, planted aloe there. Later on the father of the pianist Wim Statius Muller became the owner of San Sebastian.

The house has been privately inhabited since the mid-twentieth century. The floors are covered with yellow bricks and, to emphasize its original character, the residents have recently replaced the windows with wooden shutters.

64 | SANTA BARBARA

Around 1832 the writer Teenstra called this manor house "the largest and most beautiful house in all of Curaçao". Indeed, Santa Barbara stands out remarkably as it rises majestically from its green surroundings. A stately and lofty set of stairs leads to the living areas, and from the elevated terrace above the *mangasina's* its residents look out over the Spaanse Water and the Tafelberg.

At the end of the last century the plantation grounds were sold to a developer. There has been a lot of construction, and when the additional plans are implemented the now detached country house will be surrounded by residential areas, hotels and golf courses. The popular Barbara Beach has become a private beach for hotel guests. The oldest part of the manor house, which was built around 1800, is located in the north wing. It is perhaps a remnant of the fortified house that the Spanish governor of Curaçao, Lazaro Bejarano, supposedly built in the sixteenth century. The Santa Barbara plantation was founded by Matthias Beck, vice-president of the West India Company between 1657 and 1668. At that time cane sugar and tobacco, along with indigo, as evidenced by the discovery of indigo containers, were grown. Later, crops such as sorghum, beans, peanuts and other vegetables were added. Furthermore, there was a large amount of cattle present: sheep, goats, cows, donkeys and a few horses. The meat and milk were sold locally.

In the mid-nineteenth century nopal cacti were planted for the cultivation of cochineal lice from which the color carmine red is derived.

The manor house has had many illustrious residents and visitors. During the time that George Curiel, church warden of the Santa Ana Church, was its owner (1815-1833), Father Niewindt, for example, regularly retreated to Santa Barbara. There he read the Holy Mass every two weeks for the local population. Later other priests read mass, but this stopped when the Protestant Hendrik Schotborgh became the owner in 1833. Hendrik Schotborgh and his wife, Jeannette Kikkert, the daughter of governor Kikkert, regularly stayed in the manor house. In 1835, Prince Willem Frederik Hendrik spent the night with them during his visit to Curaçao. René Römer, who was governor of the Netherlands Antilles from 1983 to 1990, also lived at Santa Barbara for almost three years while the governor's residence in Fort Amsterdam was being thoroughly restored.

Santa Barbara is best known for the Tafelberg, where Cornelis Gorsira discovered phosphate in 1874. The Englishman John Godden began exploiting the Tafelberg in 1875. In 1912, the Curaçao Mining Company, which acquired the manor house and the plantation, was established. On the occasion of the 1953 coronation of Britain's Queen Elizabeth, the Curaçao Mining Company, with its predominantly British personnel, decided to more or less rebuild with modern materials the then dilapidated manor house. It is for that reason that this manor house is not a protected monument, but by using concrete the columns on the gallery could be set further apart. Thus the appearance has changed slightly. Following the restoration, R.J. Mesney, the director of the Mining Company, became its first occupant.

The current residents carefully restored the house in the 1990s and, if it is up to them, the house will not fall into disrepair again.

SANTA CRUZ

Sint Kruis

Santa Cruz was one of the few plantations where sugar cane was cultivated for a long time. The hull of the sugar mill on the other side of the main road bears witness to this; it is the only one on the island. Rum was distilled from the sugar for local enjoyment. During the slave uprising of 1795, the slaves made ample use of it. In the middle of the nineteenth century there was still a distillery with two boilers.

The house on this old plantation dates from the first half of the eighteenth century. There was a lot of cattle and there are remnants of pig stables. There are also three wells.

In 1866 owner, Willem van Uytrecht, relinquished a plot of land for the construction of a quarantine building when the bay of Santa Cruz was designated a quarantine berth for ships from areas plagued by contagious diseases.

In the twentieth century, shon Etie (August Georg) Statius Muller owned the plantation. There was some commotion when he closed the beach to the public in 1941. Only members of the Kwiek Sports Club were welcome.

From 1944 the country house was rented out and the beach was again publicly accessible. Following its sale in 1983, the house has been privately inhabited.

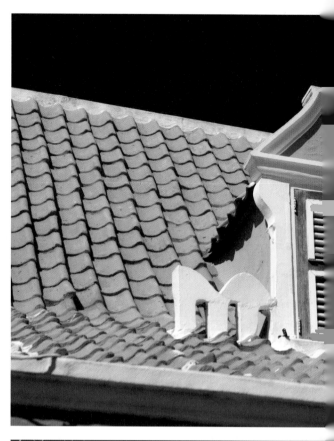

SANTA HELENA

Sainte Hélène, Plan Helena, Bijgelegen

THE STAINED GLASS WINDOW ABOVE
THE DOOR INCLUDED THE NAME OF THE
PLANTATION HOUSE: SAINTE HÉLÈNE.

About seventy years ago this small, somewhat dilapidated plantation house with a gingerbread balustrade around its porch still looked stunning. The fronton (tympanum) above the entrance showed a similar fretwork pattern. The stained glass window above the door included the name of the plantation house (Sainte Hélène) which, according to Father Brenneker, dates from 1882. Originally, the upper part of the door also had stained glass.

In 1908 Henriette Dorothea van Uytrecht, also known as shon Foochi, inherited the plantation house from her mother and namesake. Henriette married Petrus Pietersz, known also as Shon Pe, and used Santa Helena as a country retreat. In the mid 1920s, shon Foochi and shon Pe themselves lived there while their house on Frederikstraat was being expanded. Subsequently the plantation house was rented as a duplex. From 1931 until around 1953 the Bos Verschuur family lived on the right, and the Van der Jagt family on the left. The back patio was divided in half by a wall, and there were no arches yet. To the left of the house was an orchard with fruit trees where the Bos Verschuur children liked to play. In 1952, Bos Verschuur, who would go on to become the director of the National Radio Service, delivered from this house the first televised broadcast in Curaçao. In the 1980s Philip Pietersz bought the house from the estate, and it now belongs to his son.

67 | SAVONET
Sabaneta

Hundreds of goats, sheep and cows once grazed here; the fields were full of *maishi chikí* (sorghum), and owner Matthias van der Dijs experimented with nopal cacti, cotton and aloe. Those times have long passed: since 1978, the former Savonet, Zorgvlied and Zevenbergen plantations have merged into Christoffel Park where tourists and Curaçaoans enjoy tranquility and nature. The 2000-acre park is home to the endangered Curaçao deer, the *biná*. The plantation house has contained a museum since 2010.

Where at one time the Van der Dijs and Van der Linde Schotborgh families ate and slept, visitors now walk through the beautifully decorated museum rooms. Thanks to modern technology they can now get an impression of past plantation life, of the people who lived and worked around the plantation house, as well as of the Arowaks who lived here almost 4000 years ago.

Savonet is one of the oldest and largest plantations on the island. In 1660 Willem Beck was the first owner of the land which, under the ownership of Matthias van der Dijs from 1815 onward, would grow into a flourishing plantation of enormous size. In 1830, Van der Dijs bought the neighboring Zorgvlied plantation.

Marauding Englishmen set fire to Savonet's plantation house in 1805. Due to the eighteenth-century characteristics of the present country house, it is suspected that it was rebuilt in eighteenth-century style during the nineteenth century. The undulating façades, also of the dormer windows, are in any case typical of the eighteenth century.

It is noteworthy that Savonet has so many intact annexes. In addition to the *mangasina*, these are the stables, a milk house, an outhouse with room for five people, a dovecote, a forge, a little house where charcoal was stored, a foreman's house and cattle corrals. These have all been restored under the supervision of the engineering office Techcon NV. The original wooden hatch locks, called *soldaatjes* (little soldiers), were also copied.

In the past, in order to provide the residents, the fields and the cattle with water, several wells along with drinking troughs for the animals were dug nearby. These can still be seen within walking distance of the plantation house.

It is clear from the inventory that Van der Dijs, who also owned a house in Otrobanda, only lived in the plantation house part-time. Considering the enormous distance to the city that is not so strange. The family of Jacob van der Linde Schotborgh, who bought the plantation in 1863 from Van der Dijs' daughter Eva, regularly stayed in the plantation house: two of his eight children were born there.

The plantation house was a working plantation until 1963. In that year the sanatorium in town decided to stop buying milk from Savonet. The cows were sold, and the owner, Emma Van der Linde Schotborgh-Debrot, died two years later at the age of 82. The Island Territory of Curaçao then purchased both plantations in 1968 as well as Zevenbergen in order to create Christoffel Park. Initially the renovated *mangasina* served as a museum, but the restoration of the plantation house and the other annexes had to wait until 2007. Three years later, the current cultural museum opened. Thus preservationists gave Savonet a new life.

SIBERIE
Sint Joris

This is one of the few plantations in Curaçao ever owned by a Venezuelan: Silberio Cafiero bought Siberie and Jan Kok in 1784. He lived at Siberie, which was then called Sint Joris, but the plantation later took his name.

From 1830 until 1978, Siberie was owned by the Statius Muller family. August Leberegt Statius Muller, the owner of *De Curaçaosche Courant*, lived on the plantation and expanded the salt pans in the bay of Sint Marie in 1832. He also experimented with the cultivation of cotton.

Professor Went, who took stock of the state of agriculture in 1901, praised Siberie for its large herd of cattle even though he had doubts about the butter and cheese preparation.

Between 1906 and 1913 the district master lived in the eighteenth-century house. When heavy rainfall in 1906 led to the collapse of the steep roof with its eight dormer windows, it was replaced by a hipped roof over its core. This new roof has no dormer windows and does not connect to the pent roofs covering the galleries. The kitchen has an original *fornu* (oven) built out of yellow bricks.

The current owner renovated the plantation house in 2018 and retained various authentic elements. A donkey stable, with its original wooden door, and the large *mangasina* have been converted into holiday apartments.

STEENEN KORAAL

AS OF 1980 THE TEACHERS' UNION
SITEK HAS HAD ITS HEADQUARTERS
IN THIS SIMPLE PLANTATION HOUSE

In the seventeenth century Steenen Koraal was a cornfield and provided pasture for eighty goats. Until the government bought the Steenen Koraal plantation for the establishment of housing projects in the twentieth century, this goat farming remained important for the plantation for three centuries.

The previous owner significantly renovated the plantation house and also deepened the wells, installed windmills, and put up barbed wire.

After the purchase, the government made the plantation house available to the boy scouts in the 1930s. Steenen Koraal was next inhabited by various families. In the early 1970s the General Antillean Contractor Company was headquartered there.

As of 1980 the Teachers' Union Sitek has had its headquarters in this simple plantation house which is used extensively by its members. Two years earlier it had been offered for sale with the commendation that the house had been restored in its entirety and included 10,000 square meters of land. The plantation house has recently undergone another renovation.

70

SUIKERTUINTJE

Seketenchi, Chinchorro, Zuikertuin

Until the construction of the Schottegatweg in 1931, the Suikertuintje and Groot Davelaar plantations bordered each other. Between 1888 and 1936 both plantations had the same owner. They first belonged to Mozes de Marchena, and in 1906 the Winkel family assumed ownership. The Winkels enjoyed spending time in the shady orchard with its mango and sapodilla trees nestled between the plantations.

In 1932 the Winkel Company sold both plantation houses to Santos Vincente Gomez, half-brother of the Venezuelan dictator. During the Second World War, Gomez relinquished the plantation for the establishment of a recreational area for the marines stationed in Curaçao.

Gomez himself left for Costa Rica in 1936, whereupon Samuel Seikens started in the plantation house a grocery store later taken over by Toffie Hofland in 1950. After a thorough restoration of the 1870 plantation house Hofland opened the popular Toko Zuikertuintje. Busloads of American cruise tourists came to buy Dutch products there.

In 1964 a colonial styled extension was added to house a coffee bar, a bakery, and barber's shop. When the grocery store closed its doors, café De Heeren opened in 2000. The plantation house was then restored and expanded. Since 2007 the extension has housed the Zuikertuin Mall. The upper floor of the plantation house has been converted to office space.

71

URDAL

Tuintje Arrarat, Rosendal

IT SEEMS LIKE THE RESIDENTS LEFT IN A GREAT HURRY

If you didn't know it, you would never guess that there is a manor house on the Kaya Urdal. It is hidden behind tall bushes, and it seems like the residents left in a great hurry.

| 235

The cookbooks are still in the kitchen cupboard, the fan hangs on the wall and the beds can easily be slept in. And yet this small manor house has stood empty for a number of years. The wall of the façade has been partially demolished, clearly revealing its construction of coral and limestone. Luckily, the roof is still intact.

This nineteenth-century house is a typical example of a country estate. The house has no stone outbuildings unless one counts the modern garage. Next to the kitchen is a square reservoir with rounded inside corners. An additional room has been added behind the manor house.

From 1978 to 2011, the artist Ria Houwen rented Urdal. She gave drawing and painting lessons in the manor house and took care of its maintenance. The owners live in Venezuela.

72

VAN ENGELEN

Mount Vernon

Around 1700 Jan van Engelen bought the site on which the Van Engelen house was later built. It is a classic eighteenth-century manor house meaning that the core, covered by a hipped roof, has galleries with pent roofs on all four sides. The house was once surrounded by a large expanse of land, but the site was parceled out in the late 1930's whereupon it gradually lost its grandeur. It now sits abandoned at the end of a dirt road. Fortunately there is hope for the manor house because it has recently been sold.

By 1818 Van Engelen was already called "a beautiful and well-situated country retreat or plantation". This suggests that, from the outset, it was meant as a country estate, with fruit and vegetables for its own use, rather than as plantation with many products and livestock.

Nevertheless, its owner, Samuel Cohen Henriquez was very active on his plantation around the turn of the last century. According to Professor Went, who published a report on agriculture and horticulture at the beginning of the twentieth century, Henriquez experimented with sisal and hemp and set up a rope shop, although the sales of rope proved disappointing. In the 1940's, Van Engelen supplied the liqueur industry with laraha peels.

VEERIS
De Drie Gebroeders, Union

In 1722 Abraham Veeris became the owner of the De Drie Gebroeders plantation. In 1814 it merged with the Eendracht and Westerveld plantations to form the Union plantation, now known as Veeris. Incidentally, the three plantations had belonged to the same person since 1783, namely Mordechay Alvares Correa who bought them in succession.

In 1882, Johan Peter Eskildsen announced in the newspaper that he and his family would be moving to the Union plantation. Presumably they moved into the current plantation house. There Eskildsen had a large herd of cattle and grew sisal among other crops. A year later he became district master of the fourth district, and somewhat later he also became the acting district master of the fifth district. Eskildsen accomplished a lot of good for the poor and frequently opposed the plantation owners. According to him, they deliberately let their cattle run free which led to the destruction of the gardens of the needy grassland residents. Shortly before his death in 1906, he offered the plantation for sale.

The land around Veeris has since been sold for, among other purposes, the construction of the Sambil shopping center. In 2002 the plantation house was a total ruin. After a restoration and occupancy as a private residence, the house again fell into disrepair. It is now, once more, being renovated.

VREDENBERG

Kunuku Abou

From 1726 onward this country house was owned by two families and their offspring. Until 1896 it was run by the Specht family, and afterwards by the Gorsira family and their descendants.

Pieter Specht bought the plantation in 1726. Enough rainwater flowed from a nearby hill to the orchard, so fruit and vegetables flourished. The products were sold in town, as was the well water, goat cheese and goat milk. Later on this plantation and a few others were inherited by all thirteen children of Pieter's grandson Daniel and the free, colored Maria Libiana Vredenberg. The plantation did not benefit from having so many owners and gradually Vredenberg grew neglected. Apparently none of the thirteen children lived at Vredenberg, because the old plantation house was demolished somewhere between 1830 and 1842. In the descriptions the plantation with its two huts was referred to as a "garden" rather than a plantation.

The brothers Jan Hendrik and Richard Senior saved the day. They were married to two Specht sisters, and in 1846 they bought Vredenberg at a public auction. Under their management the plantation began to flourish again, due especially to an increase in the number of cattle. More than ten years later the one surviving brother built the current plantation house. Following his death, two of his sons carried on the tireless activity of the plantation.

So much for the Specht family and relatives. In 1896 the Gorsira family took charge of the plantation. In that year the merchant Herman "Mani" Gorsira purchased Vredenberg. As can be seen on a stone on the right pillar of the front gate, Herman had Vredenberg rebuilt in 1911. He moved the main entrance to the north side and mounted a beautiful balcony above it.

Herman lived with the hat braider Antonica Rosalia Steenmijn in the plantation house. Remarkably, she was the granddaughter of one of the slaves who belonged to the former owner, Jan Hendrik Specht. In 1945 Herman's oldest child, Maria Augusta, better known as shon Mimi, inherited part of the plantation along with the plantation house. She also inherited Marie Pampoen which she sold in order to maintain Vredenberg. For the same reason she built, a number of rental bungalows on the site in the 1970s. In her time goats and sheep still roamed the grounds, and there were fruit trees in the courtyard. Shon Mimi's nephew, Piet Eddine, a grandson of Mani Gorsira, inherited the plantation house in 1996 and had it restored to its former glory by the architectural firm Habibe & Maia. As part of the renovation all of the extensions made by his aunt were removed. The old kitchen was restored, complete with a *fogon* (fireplace), *fornu* (oven) and chimney. The *mangasina*, with the original floor made of flattened flint stones, remained intact, and the cistern was converted into a laundry room. The plantation house was inhabited until around 2015, and the restaurant Primas, serving local dishes, was located there until 2017. There are plans for alternate uses,and to this end the interior is being redesigned.

WACAO

The Wacao plantation house is the youngest plantation house described in this book. It is about a century old and was probably built by Gijsberto Herrera who then sold it to Bacilio Djaoen in 1927. Djaoen's great-grandchildren, the Finies, are the current owners.

The plantation itself dates to the eighteenth century. It was described as a "very suitable house … in very bad condition" when the government bought a part of Wacao in 1914. That house has now disappeared.

Until late into the last century the plantation grew millet in the rainy season. The millet was fed to the many cows and goats on the property. The cows' milk was sold to the hospital. The plantation was also famous for its *patia's* (watermelons) and there was small scale fishing. One of the Finies brothers still herds cattle, but these days the lease of the land to the Royal Netherlands Navy as training grounds is an important source of income.

The house originally had gas lighting, and the pipes are still present. Bacilio's son Jimmy Djaoen, nicknamed "Chimi di Wacawa", had three bedrooms and two bathrooms added to the house for his grandchildren who spent the weekends and holidays there. He has removed the *fornu* (oven). Unfortunately the roof of the *mangasina* has collapsed.

WECHI

Weitje, Klein Malpais

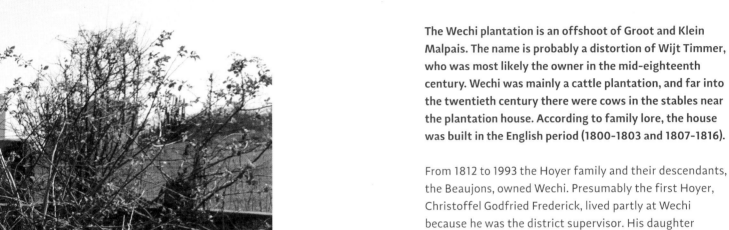

The Wechi plantation is an offshoot of Groot and Klein Malpais. The name is probably a distortion of Wijt Timmer, who was most likely the owner in the mid-eighteenth century. Wechi was mainly a cattle plantation, and far into the twentieth century there were cows in the stables near the plantation house. According to family lore, the house was built in the English period (1800-1803 and 1807-1816).

From 1812 to 1993 the Hoyer family and their descendants, the Beaujons, owned Wechi. Presumably the first Hoyer, Christoffel Godfried Frederick, lived partly at Wechi because he was the district supervisor. His daughter Charlotte and her husband, goldsmith Richard Raven, used Wechi mainly as a country retreat, while Charlotte's granddaughter Marie Hoyer, married to a Beaujon, occupied the house herself. Her son Henry moved his family to Wechi during the Second World War and afterwards used it as a country house.

During the residence of subsequent tenants, the yellow bricks on the floors of the front gallery and the *sala* disappeared under a layer of cement. In 1993 the Public Housing Foundation took ownership with the intention of constructing a new housing estate on the former plantation grounds. This plan was unsuccessfully opposed by environmentalists. The grounds have now been razed, and the allotment has begun. The plantation house has since been restored and serves as an information center.

77 | ZEELANDIA
Mount Vernon

This plantation house was already a country retreat at the end of the eighteenth century since the plantation itself was not very significant. The salt pans were so unimportant that they were not even mentioned in the mid-nineteenth century.

In 1936, the Protestant Association for Social and Charitable Work purchased Zeelandia for the establishment of the Queen Wilhelmina Home for the elderly. The large annex, with its seemingly historic façade, dates to 1945. In the early 1950s it housed the Maternity Clinic Zeelandia. The Rotary holds its weekly meetings in another new annex that connects to the plantation house. In 1966 the mansion was so dilapidated that an evening benefit was held to raise funds for its restoration. The home existed until 1983; shortly thereafter the plantation house was again restored under the direction of architect G.H. van Dortmondt, and yet again in 1999. At that time, the well-known restaurant Curnonsky was located there.

Zeelandia was built in several phases. The striking façades with spiral ornaments turned inwards (volutes) and the open galleries with columns date from the end of the eighteenth century. A century later, two wings were built perpendicular to the existing structure, probably one after the other, so that the house now has a cross floor plan. The current entrance is located in this new part, and it has a beautiful staircase.

ZUURZAK

Sòrsaka

Although Zuurzak dates from 1725, its appearance was greatly altered by an 1876 renovation in the romantic style by then owner Michael Brown Gorsira. He moved the entrance to open onto an arched gallery decorated with beautiful draperies. According to a reconstruction of its 1819 condition in Ozinga's monuments' book, the towers were by then connected by walls with battlements that are still partially present.

The *Den Dunk*i nature reserve still has old trees from the plantation as well as the bridge originally built in 1876 and restored in 2015. The story that slaves were offered for sale on the bridge can be dismissed as a myth since slavery was abolished in 1863. Zuurzak was also an indigo plantation.

The Gorsira family has long used Zuurzak as a country retreat. During the Second World War, the house was occupied by senior American officers who hosted parties and receptions there. Following a major restoration, the house served as the official residence for the lieutenant-governors of Curaçao between 1978 and 2010. The prime minister was then supposed to take up residency, but unfortunately this did not occur. In early 2018 there was a fire in the kitchen, and currently the house sits empty.

RECOLLECTIONS

CAREL DE HASETH

ANDRÉS, DAISY AND PEDRO CASIMIRI

Habaai plantation house

"IN THOSE DAYS EVERYTHING WAS VERY WELL ARRANGED."

Pedro was five, Andrés four and Daisy was yet to be born when the Casimiri family arrived from Dutch East India. They had spent the war years in a Japanese internment camp and arrived here destitute. They moved into a small wooden house at Coronet. The pastor of Pietermaai arranged for housing at the Habaai plantation house on the condition that the father would take care of the maintenance of the plantation house, and that the sons would become altar boys in the chapel of Habaai which was then a boarding school for girls. "Compared to the house at Coronet, Habaai was a palace with an enormous garden," says Andrés. "Between the plantation house and Seru Dòmi there was one large *mondi*, and behind the plantation house there was an orchard with all kinds of fruit trees."

In addition to the Casimiri family, who lived on the second floor and in the attic, there were other residents. Two old ladies lived on the ground floor, and a nursery school also occupied part of the space. In the bottom floor of the side wing there was a kindergarten, and Dominico Herrera and his two sisters lived upstairs. Finally, the architect Manders and his family lived in the rear section by the patio. "When Herrera came home from work, he would play the piano until late into the night. The piano stood next to the room where I slept and I can still hum along to that classical music," says Andrés.

When it rained, it leaked everywhere. Maintaining the house meant, among other things, that Andrés and his brothers had to climb up onto the roof to cover the tiles with cement. They also remember how the entire neighborhood came to help Truusje (their mother) whenever the house had to be painted. This was done using large buckets of lime with aloe and yellow dye.

Shon Chita lived with her son in the *mangasina* that is still there. She smoked cigarettes *kandela paden*[1]. "When you visited her, you were always offered tea and a cookie," Daisy remembers. "She kept goats, and she and her son slept in the same room with the animals. When the flames at Shell flared, the goats panicked at the sights and sounds. Their panic upset Shon Chita very much."

"The flaring from the flames was also frightening because the shadows cast on the walls looked like ghosts," says Andrés.

Andrés', Daisy's and Pedro's father kept hundreds of chickens on the property. Andrés and his brothers helped build the runs for the animals. Brouwer from the Groot Sint Michiel plantation collected the eggs. He delivered milk from his own plantation and eggs from Habaai to his customers.

There was always plenty of activity for the Casimiri children: they played war with friends in the nun's cemetery, creating tents nailed to the crosses. The old army trucks that were stored on the site formed part of their playground. There were also barracks where Portuguese ice cream vendors lived leaving their ice cream carts parked outside. And last but not least, there was swimming in the Schottegat where the nuns and the girls from the boarding school came to cool off. "Every week a Shell employee, dressed in a neat white suit and wearing a tropical helmet, would come to take water samples to check the water's quality," Andrés recalls. "In those days everything was very well arranged."

---

[1] With the burning end in her mouth.

CHRIS WINKEL

Klein Sint Michiel plantation house

"THE PLANTATION HOUSE PLAYED AN IMPORTANT ROLE IN MY PERCEPTION OF THE FAMILY"

"From the age of nine to the age of twelve I lived at Klein Sint Michiel, and later I often visited family there. We had come from the Netherlands where we lived in a houseboat in Paterswolde. By comparison a plantation house seemed huge. I lived, along with my parents, two brothers and a sister, on the top floor. Later another brother and sister were born. Siblings Chimbo en Mère[1], my great-uncle and great-aunt, lived on the ground floor. After their death, my uncle Cai lived at Klein Sint Michiel until the beginning of this century." When Chris lived at Sint Michiel, the stables were a reminder that cows had been kept there in the 1940s. At that time milk was delivered to the Curaçao Milk Plant in which Shell had some involvement. *Kesh'i buriku* (white cheese), yogurt and *kalmèki* (buttermilk) were also made there. "But in my time there was still the orchard with mango and sapodilla trees and sheep and goats. *Maishi chikí* (sorghum) and peanuts were cultivated on the *serká* (fenced part of the *kunuku*). I still remember that the terrain was plowed."

"There used to be a forest of sweetsop trees in the *ro'i santu* along the road to Bullenbaai. But all of the trees died following an oil leak from the pipes of Shell. Chimbo later had a new orchard with mango trees planted in that area. Papayas, tomatoes and eggplants were also grown."

"The plantation house played an important role in my perception of the family. You got to know all of the family members who came to visit. I also found it special that Mère and Chimbo knew almost everyone in the vicinity of Jan Doret, Samí Liber and the fishermen of Boka. Nowadays you don't see that anymore."

"As for the house itself, the *sala* with a large round table in the middle of the room was *pa nèchi* (for show) and was not used. One sat in the *hadrei* (gallery) and received visitors there. Rugs and antique weapons from the museum of Cornelis Gorsira hung on the walls.[2] There was also a television set which was a novelty at the time. We ate in the dining room adjacent to the sala and the large kitchen."

"The entrance was at the terrace on the side of the plantation house. Above the doorway was a carving of Saint Michael defeating the dragon. There was also a "slave bell" on that terrace. The front entrance with its double staircase was only used on special occasions. In the back there was also a terrace with a *baki* (water reservoir). You were allowed to swim in it under the specific condition that you would not jump into the tank. That is where I learned to swim with a snorkel and goggles. "

"Agustin, who was Portuguese, and Janu, employees on the plantation, took their meals under an awning on the back terrace. They cared mainly for the *hòfi* and the sheep and goats. In addition, you had Agustu, the overseer (*vitó*) who lived in Jan Doret, and Don Juan, a British Indian, who grew vegetables for himself on a section of the plantation, and who lived in the outbuildings below. Janu had a very small head and was rather limited intellectually, but he did tend to the orchard. Mère had cared for him for years. I remember a furious fight that Janu once had with Agustin. He shouted indignantly: 'Ta ken ta manda aki, han?!' (Who's the boss here, huh!)."

"With regard to ghosts: our maid Chel once said that Shon Djendjeres was believed to haunt the place. She was referring to Genereux Richard de Lima, a former owner. I never noticed anything myself. But what I always found striking was that everyone in the area locked their homes up tightly at night."

---

1 *Michael Brown Gorsira and Maria Catharina Brown Gorsira.*
2 *At the beginning of the twentieth century Cornelis Gorsira established a museum in the building that at present houses the island's cadastre.*

MARCEL VAN HENNEIGEN
Brakkeput Abou plantation house

"LOKE TA DEN KURÁ DI SHON, TA DI SHON"

"The fact that my parents bought the plantation house was unusual. Plantation houses were for the upper class, not for people like my parents," says Marcel van Henneigen. "It all started when Big Boy, a friend of my father's, wanted to get rid of his cows. Big Boy was a mechanic in Marchena and kept cows in the neighborhood. There they caused a nuisance so he gave them to my father as a gift. After first keeping them at Yotín Kòrtá, he looked for a different solution. That turned out to be Brakkeput Abao, which was then for sale."

"My parents took out a loan with Maduro & Curiel's Bank for the then hefty amount of 75,000 guilders in order to buy the plantation. They worked very hard to repay the loan and give their children a good education."
Those parents were James van Heyningen (upon renewing his passport, his name was written as Van Henneigen and it remained so) from Saint Maarten and the Curaçaoan Margaritha (Margo) Mercelina. James was a tailor, and his wife Margo braided hats and sold li (adelisia, a kind of water ice). In addition, the Van Henneigens had a butcher shop and market in Marchena and a coffee roasting factory at Dein. "At home, my father ground the roasted coffee, and

then we had to pour it into bags. I noticed that after every few scoops of coffee beans my father would put something else in the machine. But, of course, as a child you don't ask questions. Only later did he admit that he blended corn flour along with the coffee: it was cheaper than coffee…"
The family was comprised of the parents, four children from Shon Margo's previous marriage and three from her marriage with Van Henneigen. The household was run by Grandma Pepe, Shon Margo's mother. "We first lived on the Oranjestraat. Later my father had three houses built at Zeelandia: one for the family and two as rental properties. In the mid-1940s we moved to Brakkeput Abao." In addition to the cows with which it all started, they kept goats, sheep, and chickens on the plantation. "The goats roamed freely. They returned in the evening and were locked up in the goat corral. At times there were also kabritu shimaron, goats not from our own herd. They were usually somewhat wary, but once they were secured in the corral no time was lost. They were slaughtered the same evening and the meat was sent to the butcher shop. Loke ta den kurá di shon, ta di shon.[1] There were also about seven hundred laraha trees (orange apple trees) on the plantation. The peels of the laraha were used in the production of Curaçao liqueur. At first the peels were sold for 3.50 guilders per kilo, but the price later rose to 23 guilders per kilo. Tending to the trees, harvesting the fruit, and drying the peels was labor-intensive.

The plantation employed a lot of people from the surrounding area. "My mother was also known for her gold jewelry. My parents bought jewelry at the pawnshop, the Savings and Loans Bank. My father cleaned and repaired the pieces where necessary and then sold them. He also designed jewelry that he had made at Fèchi Regales."

"My mother was illiterate all her life. If something had to be signed, she would point to her husband and say 'Laga e ingles firma'[2], but she was sharp and enjoyed an excellent business sense. Of her it was said: Shon Margo really buys and sells everything."

"And she was nobody's fool. My parents were Catholic. In those days you paid for a place in the church, and then your name was placed on the pew. They sat at the front of the church until one of their houses burned down, and the pastor said that it was because they did business with the devil. That was the last Sunday that the family went to mass. Shon Margo would not tolerate this condemnation from the Catholic Church so the whole family became Protestant." Following the death of their parents, the heirs parceled out the plantation. Out of respect for their mother, they named the company that carried out the allotment Adelisia Resort N.V.

---

[1] Anything in the boss's yard belongs to the boss.
[2] Let the Englishman sign.

STELLA SPROCKEL

Oost Jongbloed plantation house

"A PLANTATION HOUSE REQUIRES A LOT OF MAINTENANCE. THERE IS ALWAYS SOMETHING THAT NEEDS REPAIRING."

"A plantation house requires a lot of maintenance. There is always something that needs repairing and the costs are often substantial." This is Stella Sprockel speaking, the owner of the Oost Jongbloed plantation house. "At one point the roof had to be replaced. Fortunately, the Stichting Monumentenfonds (Monuments Fund Curaçao) helped me with this repair. But when all is said and done, I have made substantial investments in the house. I doubt that young people with a family and a modest salary can afford to maintain a plantation house."

Mrs Sprockel spent her childhood on the plantation. Her father, who was a blacksmith, inherited Jongbloed from her grandfather. There was a 'shop' (a forge) on the site with - as she recalls it - a large whetstone with an enormous handle. The anvil from the forge is still behind the house.

But the main focus on the plantation was agriculture and livestock farming.

There were cowsheds and goat corrals. The milk was delivered to the nuns at Habaai and to customers in town. There was also a *kas di mulina*, a mill, just behind the plantation house, where *maishi chikí* (sorghum) was ground.

It was a carefree time. As a young girl she roamed through the kunuku in the hot sun. Her face was covered with freckles. There were several orchards: *hòfi pariba, hòfi dilanti, hòfi di Johan* (the *vitó*, or supervisor on the plantation) and Dam, the largest. There was also a dam that was once so full it looked like a lake. In those days there was no fence around the house. The house was just open and anyone could come in. On the weekends, relatives and friends from town would come to visit, and a few chickens or a goat were slaughtered for the repast.

When Mrs Sprockel got married she went to live elsewhere, but later returned to take over the plantation house. The whole plantation business is a thing of the past. A bit further away was the Hòfi Pachi Sprockel which once belonged to her older brother but it no longer exists.

"I try to maintain the house or restore it to its original state as much as possible. For instance, I have replaced the glass shutters with wooden ones. And then you notice that every window has different dimensions. Everything must be made to measure. Not just the windows, but also the curtains."

Mrs Sprockel sees the country house as a patrimony, a bit of heritage that she wants to preserve in order to keep the memory of the past and the previous owners alive. The interior decor of the house is as original as can be, and there are large family portraits. She also likes to tell stories about her family and has numerous anecdotes, such as this one about her grandfather. "Grandpère went to *tambú* parties on horseback. That was when the priests could suddenly appear and, swinging away with clubs, break up the gathering. Grandpère did not tie his horse to a tree or a fence, but to a *flaira*, a little bush. So when the priest appeared, he would jump on his horse and rush off, bush and all."

BOB PINEDO

Zuurzak plantation house

"EVERY FRIDAY EVENING WE SHOWED MOVIES FOR FAMILY AND FRIENDS ON THE BACK PORCH."

"I lived in the Zuurzak plantation house between the ages of seven and fifteen. We first lived at Scharloo on the Kaya Otto Senior. When my mother turned thirty in 1950, my father offered her a house as a present. She was allowed to choose between Zuurzak and a house at Scharloo. She did not have to think about it for long and immediately chose Zuurzak because she knew it from a photo shoot held there with her friends Ena Dankmeijer and Lenny van der Kwast soon after arriving from the Netherlands in 1940. Thus we came to move from a small house to the big plantation house."

"I have fond memories of that time. There were no *zumbis* (ghosts), but there were rats that ran in the attic in addition to large crabs in the cistern next to the house. In the evenings I had to open the tap of the cistern and close it again, and the thought of the crabs was pretty scary."

"My grandmother loved plants and was in charge of the plants at the house and the fruit trees in the orchard. The mangos, sapodillas, sweetsops, limes, and soursops were sold at the market. She also kept chickens and ducks."

Each of the five children in the family had a chore. Bob was responsible for the four windmills on the estate. Two of them supplied water to a reservoir in one of the two towers. That water was for household purposes. A third mill provided water for the fruit trees in the orchard. A fourth gave brackish water. "Every so often I also had to clean the roof gutters. I would then climb on to the roof and enjoy the view: to one side Scherpenheuvel, to the other side the salt pans of Jan Thiel. The rainwater ran from the roof into the gutters and then to a cistern. In order to use it that water was pumped to the kitchen and passed through a stone filter."

"The house is horseshoe shaped. The front *sala* was never used; instead we used the patio with the pond and its reproduction of the Venus de Milo. The patio floor was covered with red tiles. When the sun shone on them, they became boiling hot. Everyone burned their feet, but I liked lying on the hot tiles. Perhaps my back problems later in life stem from that habit?"

"Every Friday evening we showed movies for family and friends on the back porch. My father, along with his partners Fèchi Moron and Frank Brandao, owned the Roxy and Cinelandia cinemas. We picked up the films at Palais Royal. They were usually shown in the theaters the next day. Another special event was the roasting of a whole sheep at the annual barbecue which my father organized for family and friends."

"My father had a library in one of the wings of the house. There was a large round table where he and his friends played *julepe* (a card game). Their games often grew quite noisy. In this study my father also had all the volumes of the *Boletin Comercial*, the newspaper published by my grandfather, Momon Pinedo. Unfortunately, I don't know what happened to that archive after he moved out of Zuurzak in 1975."

PLANTATION HOUSE RUINS

FRANÇOIS VAN DER HOEVEN

Unfortunately, a number of Curaçao plantation houses have deteriorated into ruins. There are some remaining foundations, but others have completely disappeared. The transition from decline to ruin is difficult to determine, but the benchmark dictates that a deteriorated plantation house still shows all of the characteristics necessary for a restoration. Thus the plantation houses Brievengat, Daniel, Jan Thiel, Klein Santa Martha and Ronde Klip were well on their way to becoming ruins when they were beautifully restored.

An original restoration of a ruin is impossible. A ruin can be rebuilt, but one would then be speaking of a reconstruction. Among a number of plantation houses with only their foundation remaining there is sometimes also a *mangasina*, a storage shed for agricultural products. These mangasinas were sturdily built and some continued to be used even after the plantation house was demolished. In many cases the roofs of these mangasinas have disappeared leaving just the heavy walls standing.

Once a week, beginning in 2008, the Archeological Study Group, popularly referred to as the "Detectives", has been researching the lesser-known historical remains of Curaçao. These are usually located in undeveloped areas, locally called the *mondi*, but there are some in town.

Because of its extensive fieldwork, the Archeological Study Group was asked to undertake the chapter on ruins for this plantation house book. The collaborators are the group of photographers Anita de Moulin, Michèle van Veldhoven, Carel de Haseth and Fred M. Chumaceiro. François van der Hoeven coordinated the effort and wrote the texts in consultation with the photographers. In particular, Anita de Moulin's knowledge of the plantation houses was of immense value.

The Werbata map of 1911 is often the guideline for our detective work. This first accurate topographic map of the island shows the habitation of Curaçao prior to industrialization.

In 1906 the topographer Johannes Vallentin Dominicus Werbata from the Dutch or East Indies was commissioned to make a map of Curaçao in order to locate sites for the construction of dams to retain rainfall. To this end a map with precise contour lines was of great importance. Such contour lines are shown on the Werbata map.

In the early twentieth century plantations were still productive. The workers lived next door in small houses usually built from branches and dirt with roofs fashioned from corn stalks or palm leaves. These houses are accurately depicted on the Werbata map. A house made of natural materials is represented by a black square. If cement was used, the house is often marked in red. Due to the accuracy of the Werbata map, many of the houses can be located. They are surrounded by the remains of utensils. Best preserved are the bottles and earthenware. It is possible that such a village next to the plantation house was originally a slave village, but that was not always the case. There are indications that there were also slave villages at some distance from the plantation houses.

Of course a plantation from the colonial past did not only consist of the plantation house and a mangasina. In the vicinity of the

plantation house there were annexes such as cisterns, stables, coach houses, forges, storage sheds of various sizes, staff quarters, bakeries, pigeon turrets, bell posts and cattle corrals. There were also orchards, dams, water troughs and wells on the plantations. The Werbata map displays them all clearly.

As mentioned earlier in Michael Newton's chapter, the only structures not shown by Werbata are the indigo containers. Indigo cultivation and production was important in the seventeenth century, but over the course of the eighteenth century world prices dropped so low that it was no longer worthwhile to grow indigo on a small scale. By the time Werbata made the map, the indigo containers had not been in use for over a hundred years. That is probably why they are not shown on the map even though they are still there.

An interval of 51 years separates Werbata's first topographical map and the second completely new topographical map made by the Land Registry in 1962. Much had changed by then. As luck would have it the Registry not only indicates the individual houses in the old agricultural areas; it also shows the new dams and wells that were built after Werbata. Unfortunately, the Land Registry maps from 1982 and 1993 are much less detailed.

Fred produced accurate digital maps of the more than 550 explorations we made with the help of GPS, and François prepared the reports illustrated with many photographs taken by our photographers. These reports are distributed to interested parties, including the archaeological and anthropological institute NAAM.

We visit the ruins of known plantation houses which are sometimes difficult to reach because they are deep in the mondi. Ruins appeal to people. They might even be called romantic. You can stand in one and imagine what it must have been like when its residents were still around. The walls, often covered with vegetation, can look beautiful, but the greenery does accelerate the decline. If no action is taken, such a ruin deteriorates into a foundation buried under a pile of stones. Just removing the vegetation from the ruin helps prevent its decline and makes visits possible. The next step is consolidation. This means that with the help of cement and sometimes wood, the ruin is

stabilized so that it does not deteriorate further. So far, Zorgvlied in the Christoffelpark is the only plantation house ruin in Curaçao that has been consolidated.

We also look for foundations of plantation houses which are far less known. And finally there is the group of plantation houses that have disappeared, but there are records indicating the date and the reason for their demolition. We visit those as well, and sometimes there are still remnants to be discovered.

The plantation houses with only foundations remaining as well as the vanished country houses are included in separate lists. The group of missing plantation houses on the site of the refinery will be addressed separately.

KAS-DI-SHON NA RUWINA

From: Ku awa na wowo, Luis H. Daal, 1971 | Translation: Esty da Costa, 2019

Kaminda un tem'
tá'atin boroto, aktividat,
awó ta rèjna un silensjo
trágiko i deprimente...
Desolashón den igra 'i solo
mjentras ku tempu poko-poko
ta baj komjendoe krenchi karni
ku a kedabo.

M'a para bo dilanti,
Kas-di-shon na ruwina,
den un kunuku pashimá,
morto di sedu 'i awa;
morto di hámbr di kje traha!
Bo klòk ku ántesnan ajá
a jama hende na trabòw tur día,
awó ta muda i, di bèrdè mes,
'kampana a guli lenga'
manera nos a lanta tende.
Bo plenchi jen 'i blòwsana,
tá tur na jaga pretu
abrí den un flur kibrá,
ku jerba shimarón ta krese
i krese i kanta gaj...

E kas akí, orgujo un día
di su dóñonan, ku tambe tá'a
doño apsoluto di kunuku, waren,
doño di lèj i di moral,
doño 'i trabòw i di kuminda
i, asta, doño di e héndenan,
ku tin nan alma inmortal,
sembrá te aja bòw
den nan bordèshi stinki;
e kas akí, orgujo i arogansja,
awó ta para pluma poko-poko!

Where once there was
commotion and activity
now reigns
a tragic and disheartening silence...
The deepest desolation under the sun
while time slowly consumes
Your last vestiges.

I stood before you
Kas-di-shon in ruins
in a parched kunuku
dying of thirst, famished for work.
Your bell that once summoned people to
their daily chores
is now mute, and appears, as the saying goes,
as though the cat has really gotten its
tongue.
Your patio overrun by blue lizards
is full of black open wounds
where weeds flourish and thrive
and display their conceit ...

This house, its masters' pride
extending to their absolute ownership of the
fields
masters of law and of morality,
of labor and of food and,
masters even of people
whose immortal souls have been buried deep
under their reeking shelter;
this house, all pride and arrogance,
is slowly falling to pieces!

At one time confident, blinded,
haughty, condescending,
you were the axis of life

Un tem' sobèrbè, sjegu,
sigur, ku bo kabés den bjentu,
bo tábata un sentro 'i bida
den kunuku; sosjal, di ekonomía
i sentro tambe di kultura;
un sentro limitá,
ma sentro al fin, simía
ku bida na potensha den bo stoma.
Awe, den lus di un solo skèrpi,
bo n' tá ni sombra mes
di loke ajera bo tá'atá
i a kere di por sigui tá pa sémpr!

Manera palu grandi,
sigjendo lèj di bida i morto,
bo tambe, Kas-di-shon, mester
a baha kabés pa pálunan chikí
a subi, krese i tuma bo lugá.
Shen i binti añ' pasá,
bo n' pensa mes riba bjehés
i e bèrgwensa ku awe bo ta pasa;
despwés di tantu glorja,
di poder sin kurasón, sin alma,
atabo, sin ta manda, i solitarjo
ta kaba, slòns, tur deskwidá,
ku un lamán di tem'
i okashón di sobra pa sinta
meditá, trankil, riba bo ajera,
bo istorja i esún di tur
ku huntu ku bo tá un parti
di nos bida i di istorja tristu
o alegre i jen' i speransa
di nos mes...

Nos hubentut aktwal,
ku n' konosé doló aínda,

in the kunuku; social, pivot of the econc
as well as the hub of culture;
a limited axis, but ultimately, the core c
the seed
with vital potential in your gut.
Today, in the piercing sunlight
you aren't even the shadow
of what you were and thought yesterda
that you could continue so imperishably

Just like big trees,
who follow the laws of life and death,
you, too, Kas-di-shon, had to give way
so that small trees could
climb, grow and take your place.
About a hundred and twenty years ago
You didn't waste a thought on aging
or the mortification that you suffer todo
after such great glory,
of heartless power, lack of soul,
you stand here feeble and lonely
languishing away, shabby, neglected,
with a wealth of time
and plenty of opportunity to sit
and quietly meditate upon your past,
your history and that of all
that with you form part
of our lives and of our own sad
or happy and hopeful selves...

Today's youngsters,
who don't yet know pain,
behold the shame of your ruin;
our rebellious and humiliated youngsters
without understanding the reasons why,
see only the dark, ugly, dirty

274 |

Note: *Luis Daal wrote the poem using the spelling that was designed in 1960 by a committee of nine people, of which he was the chairman.*

mirando e bèrgwensa di bo ruwina;
nos hubentut rebèlde
i humiljá sin komprendé e pakiko,
ta mira solamente e parti
skur, mahós i shushi i malu
ku abo, Kas-di-shon,d
a hunga hopi aña na kadena.
I nan orea so ta skucha i tende
e gritu di un doló katibu,
e grítunan di rebèldía
ku nan a heredá den nan mes sángr,
kontra tur inhustisja blanku
i kontra falta 'i karidat kristján.

Pa hopi hoben chabalitu,
kada pjedra di bo karni fofo,
i kada klenku di bo plenchi,
bo stupi i pánchinan 'i bo dak,
tá mané' pipítanan sin fin
i sángr herebé i di sodó
ku a tembla i lombra un día
bòw di lus di solo, sembrá
riba un lomba di stabachi
di un di bo katíbunan!

Pa hopi hende ku nan sedu
di vingansa i odio,
ku a hecha i kría koncha kaba,
bo adrèj, bo sal', kushina,n
bentánanan kibrá, bo stupi,
ta respirá doló ku a kwaha
ku oló di odio i abuzu bjew,
abuzu, abuzu i nada mas...

I, tòg, Kas grandi riba seru,
Ka'-i-shon na dekadensha,

and evil role which you,
Kas-di-shon, have played
for years on end.
And only their ears listen and hear
the cries of a yoked pain,
the screams of revolt
which they inherited in their own blood,
against all of white injustice
and against the lack of Christian charity.

For many naive youngsters
every stone of your frail body,
and every tile of your patio,
of your pavement and of your roof,
are as infinite drops of
boiled blood and sweat
that once trembled in the sunlight
and shone, sown on a jet black back
of one of your slaves!

For many whose thirst
for revenge and hatred
developed with an innate crust,
your galleries, your rooms,
your kitchen, your broken windows,
your porches
emanate a suffering glutinous with the
stench
of old pain and cruelty
cruelty, cruelty, and nothing more ...

And, yet, big House on the hill,
Kas-di-shon in ruins,
I derive no pleasure from your misfortune,
since, if we think carefully,
you are no more and no less

ami n' por gosa bo desgrasja,
pasobra si nos pensa bon,
bo n' tá ni mas ni menos
ku solamente un fjel refleho
di bida mané' el a ser bibá,
meskós ku e imagen ku nos wowo
ta para mira den un spil
o den un awa friw i kla...

Nos t' abo, Kas-di-shon,
ku tur bo bísjonan i istorja
di tur bo gran birtutnan,
pa poko ku nan por tá'atá.
I si pa fáltanan di ajera
 - ku por tá krimen i hopi bja'
tá un kadena largu di piká,
tur día ripití di nobo - ,
kisás un nubja 'i odio sjegu
ta skuresé nos alma i pone
nos pèrdè nos kabés;
sikjera pa un kos nos tin
un danki di pagabo
i aseptá bo utilidat di antes.

Meskós ku no tin hende riba mundu,
hinteramente malu
ni hinteramente bon, sin falta,
sin nan birtut i kos bunita,
un sentro di kultura, simía bjew
bo tambe, Kas-di-shon,
den un tera dams i na prinsipjo
di un bida nobo,
ta meresé perdón...
i di nos parti e komprenshón
ku abo mes, promé b'a kai,
no kjèr o n' tribi di duna
tem' bo sobèrbja tá'a sjegabo!

than only a true reflection
of life as it was lived,
just like the image that our eyes
behold in a mirror
or in cold and clear water ...

We are your image, Kas-di-shon,
with all your vices and history
of noteworthy virtues,
as insignificant as they might have
been.
And if, due to past mistakes,
- that might be crimes and are often
more like a litany of sins,
recurring every day -
perhaps a cloud of blind hatred
our soul darkens
and makes us lose our way;
then we owe you gratitude for at least
one reason
and acknowledge your bygone benefit.

Just as there are no people in the world
who are wholly bad
nor wholly good, without faults,
without their virtues and beautiful
facets,
a center of culture, old kernel
you too, Kas-di-shon,
in virgin territory and at the beginning
of a new life,
deserve forgiveness...
and on our part the understanding
that you, before you succumbed,
didn't want to or didn't dare to show
when your pride prevented you!

Translator's Note: *Kas di shon translates literally as house of the master and kunuku stands*
for the unforgiving and arid fields that surround the plantation fields.

CHOLOMA

Choloma is one of few plantations founded in the nineteenth century. Another one is Rio Magdalena in Bándabou.

Choloma was separated from Groot Sint Joris. The plantation house was built around 1896 and consists of three adjoining building units, each with a gable roof. At the beginning of the twentieth century the Albertina Ostrich farm was established there. The birds were bred for their feathers which were in great demand by the fashion industries in the United States and Europe. At first, rich cruise tourists happily visited the farm's park to buy fans and hats embellished with ostrich feathers. After the First World War fashions changed and, consequently, the demand for ostrich feathers declined sharply resulting in the closure of the park. In the second half of the twentieth century the plantation house was abandoned and quickly fell into decline. At present a large part of the house has collapsed, and, unfortunately, we must refer to it as a ruin.

Together Oostpunt and Duivelsklip formed one of the first plantations of the West India Company. The Duivelsklip is an impressive hill with a limestone plateau near the sea.

The Duivelsklip plantation house is located inland. It is surrounded by mystery because it is inaccessible. From a helicopter it was possible to take photographs of the remains: two rectangular limestone buildings with their walls still standing. One of them is probably a mangasina while the other might perhaps have been a dwelling since there are six openings for windows and doors. Rumor has it that there was another ruin and a grave. Following the merger with the Fuik plantation, an attempt was made to extract phosphate from Duivelsklip. In or about 1908 two impressive rail embankments were partially built to transport the phosphate to Fuikbaai. These rail embankments are still in good condition even though no train has ever run on them.

DUIVELSKLIP

FUIK

The Fuik plantation is situated between the Santa Barbara and Duivelsklip plantations and borders Fuik Bay. In addition to the usual income from agriculture, it also had very productive salt pans on its border with Duivelsklip, and there are the remains of a lime kiln, landing quays and a mangasina at Fuik Bay.

The Fuik plantation house was initially a classic square house with an attic and dormer windows. Fortunately, a photograph of it has been preserved. Later on the attic level was demolished and the plantation house was outfitted with an almost flat roof that has since disappeared. Two buildings across from the plantation house had strikingly beautiful façades. The two beautifully decorated entrance gates are still eye-catching. The main gate, which has been recreated, now forms the side entrance to the Curaçao Museum. A rare bell post still stands next to the plantation house. Also adjacent to the plantation house is the Oostseinpost (signal station), upon which stood a guardhouse and an ingenious semaphore that relayed information about ships approaching Willemstad.

The ruins of Klein Piscadera plantation house are located on a hill behind Piscadera Bay. The Joubert family owned it for many years during the twentieth century. Hyacinth Joubert, who died in 1940, fully exploited the plantation. He raised cattle, for example, in order to provide milk to the Saint Elisabeth Hospital.

His son John Joubert kept the goats, but the wells were being drained by the extensive pumping of groundwater by Shell at nearby Julianadorp. His brother Egbert had a brickworks at the Jack Evertszberg. In the second half of the twentieth century Klein Piscadera and other plantation houses were rented to teachers, mostly from the Netherlands, who appreciated their beauty and enjoyed the space, the view, and the tranquility. The small plantation house consisted of three units, each with a gabled roof. The owner who followed the Jouberts did not maintain the plantation house, and it became uninhabitable. It is now a ruin.

KLEIN PISCADERA

MINA SCHARBAAI

Buena Esperanza

Mina Scharbaai is a small plantation house located in the urban district to the west of the Schottegat, close to the Sambil shopping center. It was also called Buena Esperanza. The first owner was Wilhelmina Scharbaay.

In its prime, Mina Scharbaai was a traditional-looking plantation house with a large middle section, two side galleries and an attic with dormer windows. It stands on a small hill and has a semi-circular terrace at the front and a steep staircase leading to the entrance. Most likely it was a plantation house with a small garden attached to it. A little further along there is an almost identical plantation house, Morgenster, which, although empty, is still intact. The Mina Scharbaai plantation house, however, has collapsed. Nothing is left of the roof and only the walls are still partially standing.

Jeremi

NEWTOWN

There is really no Newtown plantation house. What can be seen on the grounds of the old Lagun plantation is an industrial complex for manganese mining that dates to the end of the nineteenth century.

John Godden, who also established Newport at Fuikbaai, invested in three beautiful English-style industrial buildings and called it Newtown. The rowlike structures were so soundly built that the walls are still standing and almost all of the details and decorations are in good condition. Because the plantation was once mined and its main building used as a holiday residence until the 1950s, it was decided that this building should be counted among the plantation houses. In the twentieth century the local population referred to the principal building as the Jeremi plantation house due to its proximity to the bay of the same name. On the land registry map of 1993 the building is identified as Jeremi. The buildings and surroundings are now part of Christoffel Park.

NOORDKANT

The Noordkant plantation is located on the low and middle terrace of Curaçao's north coast and borders the Brievengat plantation to the south.

The plantation house is situated on the middle terrace and has a classic shape. It has an attic with four dormer windows. Striking are the annexes, including the kitchen with its cistern attached to the plantation house. All of this is, in turn, linked to the mangasina via a sturdy aqueduct. The year 1857 is inscribed on the façade of the plantation house. In 1982 the plantation house was still inhabited, and it was rebuilt at the end of the decade. The traditional windows and doors with wooden shutters were removed and replaced with arched openings. The openings have never been closed. Paintings on the wall indicate the plantation house was used for Halloween parties in the 1990s.

Padiki

PATRICK

Padiki could be Patrick's Indian name, but that is just a guess. Nothing is known about the first plantation house located here. Its foundation lies to the north of the ruins of the second house and is fairly close to the large mangasina.

The second plantation house was probably built in the nineteenth century. It consists of two low buildings that are perpendicular to each other. Along with two walls they form an enclosure for the courtyard. A particularly striking detail of the plantation house is the original roofing with small wooden shingles. One bedroom was tastefully decorated with a number of curved rafters, light blue walls and beautiful flooring tiles. It was adjoined by a rather modern bathroom. Around 2015 unidentified persons hung on the wall of the bedroom two small plastic crosses with flowers.

POS SPAÑÓ

Spaansche Put

This plantation has existed since the seventeenth century. It was named for a well that was near the sea. The plantation house is situated on a hill that is 75 meters high, and thus it is one of the most elevated plantation houses.

Due to this height it was impossible to dig a well close by, and that is why we see next to the house a large and sturdy cistern which is only missing its roof. The plantation house was probably abandoned when the plantation merged with Santa Cruz. Later, most of the plantation house was demolished. The western façade and a few walls, however, remained upright long afterwards. There is a good photograph taken around 1960 which shows the façade before it too eventually collapsed. The structure was built in the shape of a classic Curaçao plantation house. At a distance there is a large mangasina with a threshing floor and an annex. Altogether it forms a beautiful complex.

The Raphael plantation house dates from the early eighteenth century and is situated between Veeris, and Groot and Klein Piscadera. Raphael borders the Piscadera inlet and bears the name of one of its first owners, Rapheal Correa.

In 1852 the plantation house was purchased by William C. Jones, and for 65 years the estate remained in the hands of his descendants. In 1982 one of them, Maria Elisabeth Hartmann, took photographs of the plantation house. The plantation house was one of the most spectacular ones in Curaçao because of the nineteenth-century two-story wing in classicist style added to the front. With its position on a hill and a staircase entrance, the building enjoyed an even more imposing appearance. After the collapse of the front of the building only a number of rear rooms surrounding a courtyard remained. The overseers, Arnoldus "Shon Nolly" Willems and his wife, maintained the plantation house until the 1980s.

RAPHAEL

RIF

In the seventeenth century the West India Company founded a number of large plantations. Sint Marie was one of them. The Rif plantation was its core before becoming a separate plantation.

The plantation house is a large building with two wings. It is the second plantation house with that name. The first was located next door, but there is no longer any trace of it. Surrounding the plantation house were the familiar buildings such as a mangasina, but it was also distinguished by a bakery and a cemetery. To the east of the plantation house, along the old access road, arose a village that was inhabited until the twentieth century. On the same road there exists a large waterworks as well as a walk-in well for cattle surrounded on three sides by solidly built walls. By the 1970s the plantation house was empty, and it gradually declined Now it's a ruin.

Sint Pieter

SAN PEDRO

Originally called Sint Pieter, San Pedro is a plantation on the rugged north coast of Bándabou. The remains of the plantation house are located near the San Pedro springs, which were once necessary for its survival.

There are two springs that continuously provide water. Consequently, an oasis with coconut palms and fruit trees was created. Corrals for cattle were built around it. The cattle grazed on the low and middle terrace. The plantation house is small and has long been in ruins. For years there was a village of *kunuku houses* around the springs. Only a few of them still remain. As evidenced by an old dance floor, the orchard at the springs was rented for twentieth-century gatherings and parties. Now the owners eke out a living with some cows, goats, a small horse-riding school and the income from charges for the right of way.

Ruïne van de Plantage „San Pedro"

SANTA CATHARINA

The Santa Catharina plantation house is located on a low hill on the north coast, west of the Sint Joris Bay. It is a simple house with only one level, but that has not always been the case.

Originally it was a classic plantation house with a windowed dormer attic. The plantation house rises from a brick foundation that forms a three sided terrace with beautiful panoramic views. A number of annexes are situated below the plantation house. Until the 1980s the house, which had no running water or electricity, was rented to teachers from abroad. When the last of them left, the owner decided to put the plantation up for sale and no longer rented out the house. If only he had done so! The sale did not take place and the plantation house fell victim to decay and vandalism. It is now, just like the annexes, a ruin.

SINT HYRONIMUS

Sint Hyronimus is an old plantation in Bándabou which is located next to Savonet and Zevenbergen. The table mountain of Sint Hyronimus is the main landscape feature of the plantation.

In the foothills of this mountain, on the north side and not far from the road to Westpunt, lie the ruins of the old plantation house which was once large and classic. Partial walls of the ground floor remain. Most conspicuous are the beautiful openings which were almost certainly enclosed by artfully crafted wooden doors similar to those still found at other plantation houses. Surrounding the plantation house there was a large mangasina and a cattle corral with a beautiful, tall building whose walls still stand. On the west side there are vestiges of a former village.

ZEVEN-
BERGEN

The Zevenbergen plantation was already a ruin at the end of the nineteenth century, but what a ruin. The large main building had two full floors the likes of which were not often seen. Four walls are still standing so one can imagine what it must have looked like.

There is also a large, one-story annex that almost certainly also had a residential purpose. All of the walls of this building are still standing. A small building next to it was habitually called a "prison" but it could also have been a bathhouse. The original color can still be seen clearly on the west side of the main building. This reddish-orange color has often been applied to old plantation houses and also to kunuku houses. It is most likely that natural resources were used to create this paint color manufactured on the island. Zevenbergen has a large mangasina which,is located, however, at a considerable distance from the plantation house. In between the two structures there is a double set of indigo containers and a beautiful brick well in a *rooi* with groundwater near the surface.

Zegu

ZORGENDAL

The small Zorgendal plantation house lies hidden behind a hill not far from the Yubi Kirindongo traffic circle in Zegu. In 1800 Zorgendal was referred to as a *kanoekje*, or plot, in the lower quarter. The 1911 Werbata map displaying the plantation house shows that it was not located on a large amount of land.

In 1927 Constant Francis Schotborgh Forbes purchased Zorgendal. He had wells drilled and used the land for agriculture and animal husbandry. His grandson, Nicky Pietersz, has fond memories of the estate. The original plantation house was composed of two units with gable roofs and a square corner room with its own roof. That became Nicky's room. His grandfather had galleries added to the south and west sides, giving the plantation house the appearance of a modern villa. Following his grandparents' death, Nicky's mother occupied the plantation house for many years before selling it in 2001. It has since fallen prey to vandalism and is now a ruin.

ZORGVLIED

The ruins of the Zorgvlied plantation house are located in Christoffel Park and can be visited easily. The Zorgvlied plantation was added to the Savonet plantation in the nineteenth century.

After the plantation house was abandoned, the walls remained standing. Over the course of years the ruins were overgrown with a lush vegetation of trees and cacti. Unfortunately, the roots of this vegetation separated the walls. The park's management then decided to take matters in hand, and the Zorgvlied plantation house became the first restored ruin on the island. Unfortunately, the plants had to be sacrificed during the restoration. After a few years, the new cement became discolored and all traces of the salvage efforts disappeared. The ruin is starting to look "old" again. A footpath leads over a threshing floor past the plantation to the beautiful bell post and then along past another ruin and a mysterious row of columns back to the threshing floor. The scenic view of the north coast from the plantation house's front terrace complements the whole picture.

51

Ik bewonder
landhuizen
om hun stijl
ik haat
landhuizen
omdat ze
monumenten zijn
van onmenselijkheid
opgetrokken
met dwangarbeid
en geselslagen
-

51

I admire
plantation houses
for their style
I hate
plantation houses
because they are
monuments
of inhumanity
erected by
forced labor
and whip lashes

| 293

From: Gedichten en Gedachten 1, **Paul Brenneker** | Translation: **Esty da Costa,** 2019

SEROE KARPATA

Theresa

Lenzaam-
heid

Mariendaal
(Karpata)

Binack

13.4

Rozendaal

Neintje
Kool

Landhuis

De

Landhuis

A s

15.0

9.4

Villa
Real

10.1

Hoop

Landhuis

Gasparito

Landhuis

29.9

Israelitische
Begraafplaats

Valentijn

Landhuis

Water
reservo

Bleinheim

Water
reservoir

Water
reservoir

Z

Z

Aanlegplaats

Z

9.9

Baa
van

Landhuis

20.0

Marchena

Landingsplaats

Asiento

Baai
van

10.6

Pensionaat
Welgelegen

Valentijn

Baken

Weeshuis
Habaai

8.0

Driehoekspunt No 18
84.79 M

Seroe Domi

Baken

Schildpadden kreek
Wachthuis

Emma werf

Pompstation

Habaai

Juliana we

Santa
Lucia

Manzanilla Baai

Scho

Manzanilla Baai

Panja
aai

tia of
Baai
riksteiger

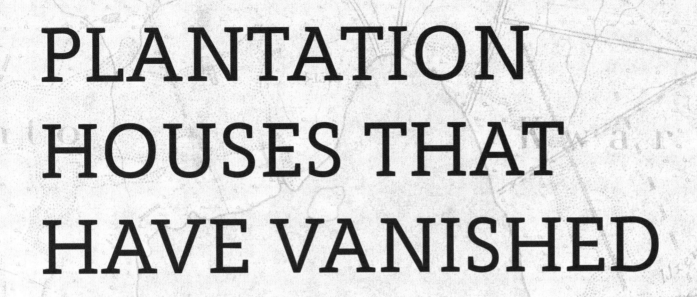

PLANTATION HOUSES THAT HAVE VANISHED

FRANÇOIS VAN DER HOEVEN

Plantation house Marchena /

At the beginning of the twentieth century, Shell bought most of the plantations around the Schottegat to allow for the construction of the oil refinery. After the plantation houses of Marchena, Gasparito, Rozendaal, Heintje Kool, Villa Real, Mariëndaal (Karpata), Blenheim, De Hoop, Valentijn, Asiento, and Rio Canario were vacated, they were demolished. The plantations and their houses such as Habaai, Groot Kwartier and Koningsplein that were adjacent to the Schottegat remained in private hands. They still exist and are discussed elsewhere in this book.

These plantation houses can all still be seen on the Werbata map of 1911 and the Werbata-Jonckheer map of 1922. On the map of 1922 the first part of the refinery, on the peninsula of Asiento, is indicated, but the now demolished plantation houses also appear.

Werbata-Jonckheer does not designate all of the houses as *plantation houses*. The criteria used by Werbata are not clear. Almost all of the "large" plantations are mentioned. The Rozendaal plantation house looks small in the photograph, but behind the small front there were several additional buildings.

The Asiento plantation house, on the other hand, which looks large in the one remaining long distance photograph is not shown. That is more understandable about the small plantation houses of Heintje Kool and Mariëndaal. The houses on the Rio Canario plantation are not drawn large enough to determine which of them functioned as the plantation house. Villa Real is a special case. Clearly indicated on a small plot of private land,

Plantation house Gasparitu

Plantation house Rozendaal

it was perhaps only used as a country retreat. Nothing further is known about this house.

In 2014 the Archeological Study Group (the "Detectives") received permission from the proprietary company *Refineria di Korsou* to explore the undeveloped areas of the refinery. That is the western area where the plantations and plantation houses of Marchena, Gasparito, Rozendaal, Heintje Kool, and Villa Real used to be located. With the help of the Werbata maps and a GPS the "Detectives"

were able to find the exact locations of the plantation houses. Shell had totally demolished them. Even the foundations had been removed. Only some debris of the Rozendaal and Heintje Kool plantation houses was discovered. Some old utensils were also found in the area.

Thus, nothing is left of this old part of Curaçao? Fortunately, the answer is yes because the beautiful Jewish cemetery Beth Haïm remains. In the seventeenth century this was the heart of the Jewish Quarter and the place where the first

Jews were granted permission to begin farming. There is another cemetery from the past that has been preserved; that is Asiento, just south of where the plantation house once stood. The small, walled cemetery is situated in the midst of industrial machinery. The "Detectives" were allowed to visit this cemetery. There are only three visible graves, one of which carries a family crest. What seems to be the case? Count Ch. A. de Larrey (1770-1832) is buried here; his wife P.E. Coerman (1779-1845) lies in the grave next to it. Who occupies the third grave is a mystery.

Plantation house Heintje Kool

Plantation house Blenheim

298 |

Plantation house Valentijn

The Tomb of Count De Larrey

PLANTATION HOUSE RUINS WITH FOUNDATIONS ONLY

An abandoned plantation house, often created by the combining of two plantations, was usually demolished in order to reuse the resulting remains as building materials. It is striking that a number of plantation house foundations have remained. Was it too laborious to remove these as well? The list of sixteen plantation houses whose foundations are still present is subject to change. The foundations could eventually disappear, and remains, usually foundations, of plantation houses might one day be unearthed. Although little is known about them, two doubtful cases have been added to the list. We are still unsure whether the "new" plantation house Spaanse Put merits this characterization, and we have not yet been able to ascertain if the Steenwijk plantation house was built atop the ruins of Coraal plantation house (Specht).

1. Bicento
2. Fontein
3. Harmonie
4. Meiberg
5. Oostpunt
6. Oranjeberg
7. Paradera - not sure yet, maybe next to the mangasina
8. Patrick - the oldest plantation house
9. Porto Marie (Port Marie, Portomari)
10. Ravenstein (Piscaderis, Vergenoeging, Donkerenberg, Blom and Hoop)
11. Rustenpad - next to Santa Cruz
12. Sint Elisabeth (Klein Blaauw) - could be razed at any time
13. Sint Joris - possibly the foundations of the oldest plantation house
14. Spijt (Spyt)
15. Wacao (Barthoolsekust, Sint Silvester) - the oldest plantation house
16. Zapateer (Buitenrust)

With more than just foundations

17. "New plantation house Spaanse Put" (Kas di Margot) - from around 1920
18. Steenwijk op Coraal - a ruin with a remarkable new house built upon it

FORMER PLANTATION HOUSES THAT HAVE DISAPPEARED

This list cannot be comprehensive because most certainly more plantation houses have disappeared than those listed here. Thus, for example, Els Langenfeld's list of "Plantages, tuintjes en kanoekjes" (Plantations, Gardens and Fields) contains countless plantations without identifying a corresponding plantation house. It might, therefore, be expected that even more will be discovered.

1. Abrahamsz – burned down in 1977, a new house was built on the site
2. Asiento – demolished by Shell
3. Blenheim (Bleinheim, Bly en Heim) – demolished by Shell
4. Bloemfontein – demolished in 2019
5. Bottelier - demolished in 2006
6. De Hoop (Jodenkwartier) – demolished by Shell
7. Dominguito (Fortuin)
8. Flip (Klein Paradera, Weltevreden)
9. Frederikslust (Rancho) –archeologically researched long ago
10. Gasparitu (Kattenberg, Klein Sint Kruis, Ma Retraite) – demolished by Shell
11. Heintje Kool (Nooitgedacht, Eenzaamheid) - demolished by Shell
12. Jongbloed – the oldest plantation house, not be confused with the Oost Jongbloed plantation house
13. Kanga (Dein, Deina)
14. Karpata (Mariëndaal)
15. Klein Davelaar - demolished to make way for the Banco di Caribe head office
16. Kleine Berg – this might be what is now known as Martha Koosje
17. Koraal Patien – a new house was built on the site
18. Lagun (Lagoen) – unknown location
19. Liverpool – unknown location
20. Mahuma (Mahoema, Luchtenberg)
21. Marchena (Buena Esperanza) – demolished by Shell
22. Maria Maai
23. Montagne Abao
24. Rio Magdalena – a new house was built on the site
25. Rozendaal – demolished by Shell
26. Rozentak
27. Rustplaats – next to Wechi, foundation razed in 2009
28. Saliña – demolished in 2013
29. San Mateo
30. Scherpenheuvel
31. Semikok – a new house was built on the site
32. Souax (Soua, Sua, Klein Mal Pais, Bon Pais)
33. Sint Jacob (Sabana Hoenkoe)
34. Tony Kunchi (Toni Koentje, Vreugdenberg) – razed in the 1960s to make way for the construction of the Toni Kunchi neighborhood
35. Valentijn (Ravenstein, Starckenborgh, Brakkesmit) – demolished by Shell
36. Waterloo – a new house was built on the site
37. Zorgvlied (Korporaal) near Jan Kok/ Hermanus – a new house was built on the site

Westpunt

Knip

Playa Jeremi

Santa Cruz

Sint ▲
Christoffelberg

Savonet

Barber

Soto

Ascencion

Santa Martha

San Juan

Cas Abao

St.Willibrodus

Bullenbaai

300 |

Plantation Houses:

1. Ascencion
2. Barber
3. Bever
4. Blauw
5. Bloemhof
6. Bloempot
7. Bona Vista
8. Bonam
9. Brakkeput Abou
10. Brakkeput Ariba
11. Brakkeput Meimei
12. Brievengat
13. Cas Abou
14. Cas Cora
15. Cerito
16. Chobolobo
17. Daniel
18. De Goede Hoop
19. De Hoop
20. Dokterstuin
21. Gaito
22. Girouette
23. Granbeeuw
24. Groot Davelaar
25. Groot Kwartier
26. Groot Piscadera

27. Groot Santa Martha
28. Groot Sint Joris
29. Groot Sint Michiel
30. Grote Berg
31. Habaai
32. Hato
33. Hel
34. Hermanus
35. Jan Kok
36. Jan Sofat
37. Jan Thiel
38. Janwe
39. Joonchi
40. Kas Chikitu
41. Klein Bloemhof
42. Klein Kwartier
43. Klein Santa Martha
44. Klein Sint Joris
45. Klein Sint Michiel
46. Knip / Kenepa
47. Koningsplein
48. Koraal Tabak
49. Morgenster
50. Mount Pleasant / Malpais
51. Oost Jongbloed
52. Pannekoek

53. Papaya
54. Parera
55. Pos Cabai
56. Ronde Klip
57. Rooi Catootje
58. Rust en Vrede
59. Saliña Abou
60. Saliña Ariba
61. San Juan
62. San Nicolas
63. San Sebastian
64. Santa Barbara
65. Santa Cruz
66. Santa Helena
67. Savonet
68. Siberie
69. Steenen Koraal
70. Suikertuintje
71. Urdal
72. Van Engelen
73. Veeris
74. Vredenberg
75. Wacao
76. Wechi
77. Zeelandia
78. Zuurzak / Sòrsaka

Ruins:

A. Choloma
B. Duivelsklip
C. Fuik
D. Klein Piscadera
E. Mina Scharbaai
F. Newtown / Jeremi
G. Noordkant
H. Patrick
I. Pos Spañó
J. Raphael
K. Rif
L. San Pedro
M. Santa Catharina
N. Sint Hyronimus
O. Zevenbergen
P. Zorgendal
Q. Zorgvlied

N
W · O
Z

25   14   23
21   71   72
3   57   41   19
55   70   7
47   6   58   42
24   5   39
15   22
77
18
16   60
54   38
33   59
74

Curaçao
International
Airport

Playa Canoa

32
76 P   G
69
29   12
Julianadorp   56
45   8   M
26   51
4 D J 49
73 E   48
40 31   23   Santa Rosa
66   28   A
    44
WILLEMSTAD   Montaña
78 Brakkeput
37
9 11 10 36
64 Spaanse Water
Jan Thiel   C
Caracasbaai   Santa Barbara   B
Fuikbaai

Oostpunt

Bibliography:

- Baetens, Eddy en Charles do Rego (2009). *Santa Martha Grandi. Het verhaal van een plantage*. Curaçao: Fundashon Tayer Soshal Santa Martha.
- Beaujon, Japa (1991). Koloniale jeugdherinneringen. In: *Drie Curaçaose schrijvers in veelvoud. Boelie van Leeuwen Tip Marugg Frank Martinus Arion*. Zutphen: Uitgeverij de Walburgpers b.v.
- Braakman, Ireen (2005). Plantage Gerustheid. In: *Kristòf*. Mei 2005.
- Bosch G.B. (1829, 1836, 1843). *Reizen in West-Indië, en door een gedeelte van Zuid- en Noord-Amerika*. 3 delen. Utrecht.
- Brusse, A.T. (1882, herdruk 1969). *Curaçao en zijne bewoners*. Amsterdam: S. Emmering.
- Dahlhaus, G.J.M. (1924). *Monseigneur Martinus Joannes Niewindt Eerste Apostolisch Vicaris van Curaçao. Een levensschets 27 aug. 1824-12 jan. 1860*. Curaçao: Apostolisch Vicariaat.
- Dissel, S. van (1857). Curaçao. *Herinneringen en Schetsen*. Leiden: A.W. Sythoff
- Ditzhuijzen, Jeannette van (1996). *Nederlandse Antillen*. Amsterdam: Uitgeverij de Arbeiderspers.
- Ditzhuijzen, Jeannette van (2010). *ENA Een leven tussen boeken*. Curaçao: S.A.L. Maduro Stichting.
- Ditzhuijzen, Jeannette van (2012). *Geschiedenis in steen. De ontwikkeling van de monumentenzorg op Curaçao*. Amsterdam: KIT Publishers.
- Ditzhuijzen, Jeannette van (2015). *Anyway... Sergio Leon, vrouwenarts en eilandskind*. Utrecht: LM Publishers.
- Ditzhuijzen, Jeannette van en Els Langenfeld (2007), 'Slaven deden zelf mee aan het systeem.' In: *Historisch Nieuwsblad*, nr. 5, 2007.
- Emmanuel, Isaac S. (1957). *Precious Stones of the Jews of Curaçao – Curaçoan Jewry 1656-1957*. New York: Bloch Publishing Company.
- Fonk, Hans e.a. (1999). *Curaçao Architectural Style*. Curaçao: Stichting Curaçao Style.
- Fonk, Hans e.a. (2004). *Curaçao Caribische architectuur & stijl*. Curaçao: Stichting Curaçao Style.
- Gaay Fortman, B. de. Benjamin de Sola. In: *Westindische Gids*, Jaargang 14, 1932-1933, p. 347-354.
- Gehlen, Gerda (2004). Geschiedenis van de plantage Damasco, alias Jan Thiel. Bijlage *Archiefvriend* jaargang 15, nr. 3, 1-8.
- Gibbes, F.E. , N.C. Römer- Kenepa en M.A. Scriwanek (2015). *De Curaçaoënaar in de Geschiedenis 1499-2010*. Curaçao: Stichting Nationale Geschiedenis.
- Gomes Casseres, Ch. (1990). *Istoria Kortiku di Hudiunan di Korsou*. Curaçao: uitgeverij Amigoe.
- De graven van Habaai (1944). In: *Amigoe*, 4 november 1944.
- Hartog, dr. Joh. (1961), *Curaçao. Van Kolonie tot Autonomie* (deel 1). Oranjestad: D.J. de Wit.
- Hartog, dr. Joh. (1961). *Curaçao. Van Kolonie tot Autonomie* (deel II). Oranjestad: D.J. de Wit.
- Hartog, dr. Joh. (1962). *Het verhaal der Maduro's en Foto-album van Curaçao 1937-1962*. Aruba: D.J. de Wit.
- Hartog, dr. Joh. (1970). *Mogen de eilanden zich verheugen. Geschiedenis van het protestantisme op de Nederlandse Antillen*. Curaçao: uitgave van de Kerkenraad van de Verenigde Protestantse Gemeente Curaçao.

- Heiligers, Bernadette (2001). *Samen leven Curaçao in de twintigste eeuw*. Curaçao: uitgeverij Amigoe.
- Hendrikse, Norbert (2005). *Hollands glorie in de kolonie*. Curaçao: Omni Media.
- Hendrikse, Norbert (2009). Landhuis Weitje Een juweeltje van Klein Malpais. In: *Antilliaans Dagblad*.
- Huijgers, Dolf en Lucky Ezechiëls (1992). *Landhuizen van Curaçao en Bonaire*. Amsterdam: Persimmons Management B.V.
- Jong, Ton de (2016). Oudste plattegrond plantage ontdekt. In: *Antilliaans Dagblad*, 16 januari 2016.
- Jonkhout-Gehlen, Gerda (2003). *Monumenten hersteld. Gerestaureerde monumenten met medewerking van de Stichting Monumentenfonds Curaçao in de jaren 1994-1998*. Curaçao: stichting Monumentenfonds Curaçao.
- John Jonkhout (2010). De eerste eigenaren van de plantage Papaya. In: *Archiefvriend*, september 2010, Jaargang 16, nummer 3.
- Kamerbeek, E.A.J. (1995), *Landhuis Ascencion*. Curaçao: Stichting Vrienden van Ascencion.
- Krafft, dr. ds. A.J.C. (1951). *Historie en oude families van de Nederlandse Antillen Het Antilliaans Patriciaat*. 's Gravenhage: Martinus Nijhoff.
- Krogt, Peter van (2005). J.V.D. Werbata, een topograaf uit Oost-Indië, karteert in West-Indië. In: *Caert Thresoor*, tijdschrift voor de Geschiedenis van de Kartografie. 24ste jaargang, 2005-1.
- Langenfeld, Henk en Els (1996). *Groot Davelaar En den Plantage Welgelegen (1732-heden)*. Curaçao.
- Langenfeld, Els. De plantage Vredenberg 1 en 2. In: *Antilliaans Dagblad*.
- Langenfeld, Els. De parochie Barber. In: *Antilliaans Dagblad*.
- Langenfeld, Els. Landhuis Vriendenwijk. In: *Antilliaans Dagblad*.
- Langenfeld, Els. Wie kan voorspellen wat ieders lot in de wereld zal zijn. In: *Antilliaans Dagblad*. 16/9/2008
- Langenfeld, Els (2007). De plantage Pannekoek 1 en 2. In: *Antilliaans Dagblad*.
- Langenfeld, Els (2004). *The Past: a Present for our Future 30 Years S.A.L. (Mongui) Maduro Foundation*. Curaçao: S.A.L. Mongui Maduro Foundation
- Langenfeld, Els (2005). *Vrij, maar toch geknecht. Het leven in Bándabou na de emancipatie*. Curaçao, ongepubliceerd manuscript.
- Langenfeld, Els (2009). Van Malpais tot Wechi. In: *Antilliaans Dagblad*.
- Langenfeld, Els (2009). De slaven van Wechi. In: *Antilliaans Dagblad*.
- Langenfeld, Els (2010). *Verhalen uit het Verleden, deel 2*. Curaçao: uitgave in eigen beheer.
- Langenfeld, Els (2011). *Lodewijk Wilhelm Statius van Eps. Een leven in dienst van de medische wetenschap*. Curaçao: privé-uitgave van de familie.
- Langenfeld, Els. *Plantages, tuinen en 'kanoekjes' met hun eigenaren. 1780-1855*. Curaçao: uitgave in eigen beheer.
- Leijdesdorff, Hans (2019). *Perrets of the Caribbean The Descendants of Moïse Perret Gentil (1725-1788) and his Son Abraham*. Curaçao: Blenchi Books.
- Maduro-Molhuijsen, Helma (2010). Savonet, vier artikelen. In: *Antilliaans Dagblad*, november 2010.

- Newton, Michael A. (1986). *Architektuur en bouwwijze van het Curaçaose landhuis*. Delft: Technische Universiteit Delft, Werkgroep Restauratie; heruitgave 1990
- Monsanto, Christel (2006). Kleine Kroniek van de plantage San Sebastiaan. In: *Archiefvriend* jaargang 12, nr. 3.
- Muller, H. P. N. (1905). *Door het land van Columbus, Een reisverhaal ....; Haarlem: Erven Bohn*.
- Noord, Sandra van, red. (2017). *Kas di Shon Plantagehuizen op Curaçao vroeger en nu*. Volendam: LM Publishers.
- Oversteegen, J.J. (1994). *In het schuim van grauwe wolken. Het leven van Cola Debrot tot 1948*. Amsterdam: uitgeverij Meulenhoff.
- Ozinga, prof. M.D. (1959), *De monumenten van Curaçao in woord en beeld*. Curaçao: Stichting Monumentenzorg Curaçao.
- Paddenburgh, G.G. van (1819). *Beschrijving van het eiland Curaçao en onderhoorige eilanden. Uit onderscheidene stukken, bijdragen en opmerkingen opgemaakt door een bewoner van dat eiland*. Haarlem: Erven François Bohn.
- Pruneti Winkel (1987). *Scharloo. A nineteenth century quarter of Willemstad, Curaçao: historical architecture and its background*. Florence: Edizioni Poligrafico Florentino.
- Rego, Charles do en Lionel Janga (2009). *Slavery and Resistance in Curaçao. The Rebellion of 1795*. Curaçao: Fundashon Parke Nashonal.
- Reilly, William Benedict (1898). Curaçao Dutch West Indies. In: *The Monthly Illustrator*, Juni 1898.
- Renkema, dr. W.E. (1981). *Het Curaçaose plantagebedrijf in de negentiende eeuw*. Zutphen: De Walburg Pers.
- Renkema, dr. W.E. (2016). *Kaarten van de Nederlandse Antillen. Curaçao, Aruba, Bonaire, Saba, Sint Eustatius en Sint Maarten tot 1900*. Leiden/Boston: Brill | Hes & De Graaf.
- Rupert, Linda M. (1999). *Roots of our Future. A Commercial History of Curaçao*. Curaçao: Curaçao Chamber of Commerce & Industry.
- Rutten, A.M.G. (1989). *Apothekers en chirurgijns Gezondheidszorg op de Benedenwindse Eilanden van de Nederlandse Antillen in de negentiende eeuw*. Assen/Maastricht: Van Gorcum.
- Simons, G.J. (1868). *Beschrijving van het eiland Curaçou, uit verschillende bronnen bijeenverzameld*. Oosterwolde: G.S. de Tempe.
- Soest, Jaap van (1975). Sisal in Curaçao: an experiment that failed (1896-1925). In: *Boletín de Estudios Latinoamericanos y del Caribe*, p. 88-111.
- Stedman, J.G. (1799-1800). *Reize naar Suriname, en door de binnenste gedeelten van Guiana*. deel 1-4, Amsterdam: Johannes Allart.
- Teenstra, M.D. (1836/7), *De Nederlandsche West-Indische Eilanden*. Amsterdam: C.G. Sulpke; heruitgave 1977.
- Velden, B.D. Van der. *Habaail Habai; Habay: Welgelegen*.
- Visman, M.A. (1976/77). De geschiedenis van landhuis Jan Kock. In: *Waya* jaargang 1 en 2.
- Visman, M.A. (1981). Van slaaf tot plantagehouder Een aspect van het 18e-eeuws plantagewezen op Curaçao. In: *Nieuwe West-Indische Gids*, 55ste jaargang, No.1, 2 p. 39-51.
- Visman, M.A. (1981/82/83). De herkomst van onze streek- en plantagenamen. In: *Waya* februari 1981 – december 1983.

Colophon:

Plantation Houses of Curaçao - Jewels of the Past published by Stichting Curaçao Style in collaboration with Stichting LM Publishers

Photography:
Plantation Houses   Ton Verkuijlen
    Brett Russel

History   Michael A. Newton

Ruins   Anita de Moulin
    Michèle van Veldhoven
    Carel de Haseth
    and others

Text:
Plantation Houses   Jeannette van Ditzhuijzen

History   Michael A. Newton

Ruins   François van der Hoeven

Interviews   Carel de Haseth

Translator   Esty da Costa

Editors   Nicole Henriquez
    Lusette Verboom
    Carel de Haseth
    Ellen Spijkstra
    Anko van der Woude
    Anita de Moulin
    Gerda Gehlen
    Rebecca Harlan

Project Coordinator: Ellen Spijkstra

Graphic Design: Salt (Carl Ariza)

Production: Hightrade B.V.

Distribution: Stichting Curaçao Style: Curaçao
    Stichting LM Publishers:
    the Netherlands, USA

ISBN: 978-94-6022-525-3

Sponsors:

The dissemination of our cultural heritage, both in Curaçao as well as beyond our borders, through a guaranteed purchase, is of great importance for our foundation. For this we thank:

Persimmons B.V./Dolf Huijgers
Trustmoore (Curaçao) N.V.
ORCO Bank. N.V.
The Beach House
Intertrust Group B.V.
Fundashon Bon Intenshon
Bruna
Maduro & Curiel's Bank N.V.
Caribbean Business Advisors
Soliana Bonapart & Aardenburg
Zuikertuintje Mall